Archie Forbes defies Sir John Kerr.—Page 35.

—In Freedom's Cause.

IN FREEDOM'S CAUSE.

A STORY OF WALLACE AND BRUCE.

By G. A. HENTY,

Author of "Bonnie Prince Charlie," "The Lion of the North," "With Clive in India," "The Young Carthaginian," "The Dragon and the Raven," "With Lee in Virginia," "By Pike and Dyke," "Captain Bayley's Heir," "By England's Aid," "Under Drake's Flag," "In the Reign of Terror," etc.

ILLUSTRATED BY GORDON BROWNE.

ISBN 0-88019-178-3

Schmul Publishing Co., Inc.
Wesleyan Book Club   Salem, Ohio
1985

Printed by
Old Paths Tract Society Inc.
Shoals, Indiana 47581

PREFACE.

My Dear Lads: There are few figures in history who have individually exercised so great an influence upon events as William Wallace and Robert Bruce. It was to the extraordinary personal courage, indomitable perseverance, and immense energy of these two men that Scotland owed her freedom from English domination. So surprising were the traditions of the feats performed by these heroes that it was at one time the fashion to treat them as belonging as purely to legend as the feats of St. George or King Arthur. Careful investigation, however, has shown that so far from this being the case, almost every deed reported to have been performed by them is verified by contemporary historians. Sir William Wallace had the especial bad fortune of having come down to us principally by the writings of his bitter enemies, and even modern historians, who should have taken a fairer view of his life, repeated the cry of the old English writers that he was a bloodthirsty robber. Mr. W. Burns, however, in his masterly and exhaustive work, "The Scottish War of Independence," has torn these calumnies to shreds, and has dis-

played Wallace as he was, a high-minded and noble
patriot. While consulting other writers, especially
those who wrote at the time of or but shortly after
the events they record, I have for the most part
followed Burns in all the historical portions
of the narrative. Throughout the story, therefore, wherein it at all relates to Wallace,
Bruce, and the other historical characters, the
circumstances and events can be relied upon as
strictly accurate, save only in the earlier events of
the career of Wallace, of which the details that
have come down to us are somewhat conflicting,
although the main features are now settled past
question.

Yours very sincerely,

G. A. Henty.

CONTENTS.

CONTENTS.

IN FREEDOM'S CAUSE.

CHAPTER XIV.

COLONSAY.

ARCHIE, having little else to do, spent much of his time in fishing. As a boy he had learned to be fond of the sport in the stream of Glen Cairn; but the sea was new to him, and whenever the weather permitted he used to go out with the natives in their boats. The Irish coast was but a few miles away, but there was little traffic between Rathlin and the mainland. The coast there is wild and forbidding, and extremely dangerous in case of a northerly gale blowing up suddenly. The natives were a wild and savage race, and many of those who had fought to the last against the English refused to submit when their chiefs laid down their arms, and took refuge in the many caves and hiding-places afforded in the wild and broken country on the north coast.

Thus no profitable trade was to be carried on with the Irish mainland. The people of Rathlin were themselves primitive in their ways. Their wants were few and easily satisfied. The wool of their flocks furnished them with clothing, and they raised sufficient grain in sheltered spots to supply them with meal, while an abundance of food could be always obtained from the sea. In fine weather they took more than sufficient for their needs, and dried the overplus to serve them when the winter winds kept their boats from putting out. Once or twice in the year their largest craft, laden with dried fish, would make across to Ayr, and there disposing of its cargo would bring back such articles as were needed, and, more precious still, the news of what was passing in the world, of which the simple islanders knew so little.

Even more than fishing, Archie loved when the wind blew wildly to go down to the shore and watch the great waves rolling in and dashing themselves into foam on the rocky coast. This to him was an entirely new pleasure, and he enjoyed it intensely. Perched on some projecting rock out of reach of the waves, he would sit for hours watching the grand scene, sometimes alone, sometimes with one or two of his comrades. The influx of a hundred visitors had somewhat straightened the islanders, and the fishermen were forced to put to sea in weather when they would not ordinarily have launched their boats, for in the winter they seldom ventured out unless the previous season had been unusually bad, and the stores of food laid by insufficient for winter consumption. Archie generally went out with an old man, who with two grown-up sons owned a boat. They were bold and skillful fishermen, and often put to sea when no other boat cared to go out.

Archie in the Isle of Rathlin.—Page 228.

—*In Freedom's Cause.*

One evening the old man, as usual before going to sea, came into the hut which Archie and Sir James Douglas inhabited, and told him that he was going out early next morning. "Fish are scarce," he said, "and it would be a disgrace on us islanders if our guests were to run short of food."

"I shall be ready, Donald," Archie replied, "and I hope we shall have good sport."

"I can't see what pleasure you take, Sir Archie," the young Douglas said when the fisherman had left, "in being tossed up and down on the sea in a dirty boat, especially when the wind is high and the sea rough."

"I like it best then," Archie replied; "when the men are rowing against the wind, and the waves dash against the boat, and the spray comes over in blinding showers, I feel very much the same sort of excitement as I do in a battle. It is a strife with the elements instead of with men, but the feeling in both cases is akin, and I feel the blood dancing fast through my veins and my lips set tightly together, just as when I stand shoulder to shoulder with my retainers, and breast the wave of English horsemen."

"Well, each to his taste, I suppose," Douglas said, laughing; "I have not seen much of war yet, and I envy you with all my heart the fights which you have gone through; but I can see no amusement in getting drenched to the skin by the sea. I think I can understand your feeling, though, for it is near akin to my own when I sit on the back of a fiery young horse, who has not yet been broken, and feel

him battle with his will against mine, and bound
and rear, and curvet in his endeavors to throw me,
until at last he is conquered and obeys the slightest
touch of the rein."

"No doubt it is the same feeling," Archie replied;
"it is the joy of strife in another form. For myself, I own I would rather fight on foot than on
horseback; I can trust myself better than I can
trust my steed, can wheel thrice while he is turning
once, can defend both sides equally well; whereas
on horseback, not only have I to defend myself but
my horse, which is far more difficult, and if he is
wounded and falls I may be entangled under him
and be helpless at the mercy of an opponent."

"But none acquitted them better on horseback at
Methven than you did, Sir Archie," the young
fellow said admiringly. "Did you not save the
king, and keep at bay his foes till your retainers
came up with their pikes and carried him off from
the center of the English chivalry?"

"I did my best," Archie said, "as one should
always do; but I felt even then that I would rather
have been fighting on foot."

"That is because you have so much skill with
your weapon, Sir Archie," Douglas said. "On
horseback with mace or battle-axe it is mainly a
question of sheer strength, and though you are very
strong there are others who are as strong as you.
Now, it is allowed that none of the king's knights
and followers are as skillful as you with the sword,
and even the king himself, who is regarded as the

second best knight in Europe, owns that on foot and with a sword he has no chance against you. That we all saw when you practiced for the amusement of the queen and her ladies in the mountains of Lennox. None other could even touch you, while you dinted all our helmets and armor finely with that sword of yours. Had we continued the sport there would not have been a whole piece of armor among us save your own harness."

Archie laughed. "I suppose, Douglas, we all like best that in which we most excel. There are many knights in the English army who would assuredly overthrow me either in the tilting ring or in the field, for I had not the training on horseback when quite young which is needed to make a perfect knight, while I had every advantage in the learning of sword-playing, and I stick to my own trade. The world is beginning to learn that a man on foot is a match for a horseman—Wallace taught Europe that lesson. They are slow to believe it, for hitherto armed knights have deemed themselves invincible, and have held in contempt all foot-soldiers. Stirling, and Falkirk, and Loudon Hill have taught them the difference, but it will be a long time before they fairly own a fact so mortifying to chivalry; but the time will come, be well assured, when battles will be fought almost with infantry alone. Upon them the brunt of the day will fall, and by them will victory be decided, while horsemen will be used principally for pursuing the foe when he is broken, for covering the retreat of infantry by desperate charges, or by charging into the midst of a fray when the infantry are broken."

"All the better for Scotland," James Douglas said cheerfully. "We are not a nation of horsemen, and our mountains and hills, our forests and morasses, are better adapted for infantry than cavalry; so if ever the change you predict come to pass we shall be gainers by it."

At daybreak next morning Archie went down to the cove where his friend the fisherman kept his boat. The old man and his two sons were already there, but had not launched their craft.

"I like not the look of the weather," the fisherman said when Archie joined him. "The sky is dull and heavy, the sea is black and sullen, but there is a sound in the waves as they break against the rocks which seems to tell of a coming storm. I think, however, it will be some hours before it breaks, and if we have luck we may get a haul or two before it comes on."

"I am ready to go or stay," Archie said; "I have no experience in your weather here, and would not urge you against your own judgment, whatever it be; but if you put out I am ready to go with you."

"We will try it," the fisherman said, "for food is running short; but we will not go far from the shore, so that we can pull back if the weather gets worse."

The boat was soon launched, the nets and oars were already on board, and they quickly put out from the shore. The boat carried a small square sail, which was used when running before the wind. In those days the art of navigation was in its infancy, and the art of tacking against a wind had scarcely begun to be understood; indeed, so high were the ships out of water, with their lofty poops and forecastles, that it was scarce possible to sail them on a wind, so great was the leeway they made. Thus when contrary winds came mariners anchored and waited as patiently as they might for a change, and a voyage to a port but two days' sail with a favoring wind was a matter of weeks when it was foul.

After rowing a mile from land the nets were put out, and for some time they drifted near these. From time to time the old fisherman cast an anxious eye at the sky.

"We must get in our nets," he said at last decidedly; "the wind is rising fast, and is backing from the west round to the south. Be quick, lads, for ere long the gale will be on us in its strength, and if 'tis from the south we may well be blown out to sea."

Without a moment's delay the fishermen set to work to get in the nets, Archie lending a hand to assist them. The younger men thoroughly agreed in their father's opinion of the weather, but they knew too well the respect due to age to venture upon expressing an opinion until he had first spoken. The haul was a better one than they had expected, considering that the net had been down but two hours.

"'Tis not so bad," the fisherman said, "and the catch will be right welcome—that is," he added as he looked toward the land, "if we get it safely on shore."

The wind was now blowing strongly, but if it did not rise the boat would assuredly make the land. Archie took the helm, having learned somewhat of the steering on previous excursions, and the three fishermen tugged at the oars. It was a cross sea, for although the wind now blew nearly in their teeth, it had until the last half hour been from the west, and the waves were rolling in from the Atlantic. The boat, however, made fair progress, and Archie began to think that the doubts of the fishermen as to their making the shore were in no wise justified, when suddenly a gust, far stronger than those they had hitherto met, struck the boat.

"Keep her head straight!" the fishermen shouted. "Don't let the wind take it one side or the other. Stick to it, boys; row your hardest; it is on us now and in earnest, I fear."

The three men bent to their oars, but Archie felt that they were no longer making headway. The boat was wide and high out of the water; a good sea boat, but very hard to row against the wind. Although the men strained at the oars, till Archie expected to see the tough staves crack under their efforts, the boat did not seem to move. Indeed it appeared to Archie that in the brief space when the oars were out of the water the wind drove her further back than the distance she had gained in the last stroke. He hoped, however, that the squall was merely temporary, and that when it subsided there would still be no difficulty in gaining the land. His hope was not realized. Instead of abating, the wind appeared each moment to increase in force. Clouds of spray were blown on the top of the waves, so that at times Archie could not see the shore before him. For nearly half an hour the fishermen struggled on, but Archie saw with dismay that the boat was receding from the shore, and that they had already lost the distance they had gained before the squall struck them. The old fisherman looked several times over his shoulder.

" It is of no use," he said at last ; " we shall never make Rathlin, and must even run before the gale. Put up the helm, young sir, and take her round. Wait a moment till the next wave has passed under us—now !" In another minute the boat's head was turned from land, and she was speeding before the gale.

" In with your oars, lads, and rig the mast, reef down the sail to the last point ; we must show a little to keep her dead before the wind ; we shall have a tremendous sea when we are once fairly away from the shelter of the island. This gale will soon knock up the sea, and with the cross swell from the Atlantic it will be as much as we can do to carry through it."

The mast was stepped and a mere rag of sail hoisted, but this was sufficient to drive the boat

through the water at a great speed. The old fisherman was steering now, and when the sail was
hoisted the four men all gathered in the stern of the
boat.

"You will go between Islay and Jura, I suppose,"
one of the younger men said.

"Ay," his father said briefly; "the sea will be
too high to windward of Islay."

"Could we not keep inside Jura?" Archie suggested; "and shelter in some of the harbors on
the coast of Argyle."

"Ay," the old man said; "could we be sure of
doing that it would be right enough, but, strong as
the wind is blowing her, it will be stronger still
when we get in the narrow waters between the
islands and the mainland, and it would be impossible
to keep her even a point off the wind; then if we
missed making a harbor we should be driven up
through the Strait of Corrievrekan, and the biggest
ship which sails from a Scottish port would not
live in the sea which will be running there. No,
it will be bad enough passing between Islay and
Jura; if we get safely through that I shall try to
run into the narrow strait between Colonsay and
Oronsay; there we should have good and safe
shelter. If we miss that, we must run inside Mull
—for there will be no getting without it—and either
shelter behind Lismore island far up the strait, or
behind Kerara, or into the passage to Loch Etive."

"It will not be the last, I hope," Archie said.
"for there stands Dunstaffnage castle, and the lands

all belong to the MacDougalls. It is but two months back I was a prisoner there, and though I then escaped, assuredly if I again get within its walls I shall never go out again. As well be drowned here."

"Then we will hope," the fisherman said, "that 'tis into some other harbor that this evil wind may blow us; but as you see, young sir, the gale is the master and not we, and we must needs go where it chooses to take us."

Fiercer and fiercer blew the gale; a tremendous cross sea was now running, and the boat, stout and buoyant as she was, seemed every moment as if she would be engulfed in the chaos of water. Small as the sail had been it had been taken down and lashed with ropes to the yard, so that now only about three square feet of canvas was set.

"We can show a little more," the fisherman shouted in Archie's ear, "when we get abreast of Islay, for we shall then be sheltered from the sea from the west, and can run more boldly with only a following sea; but till we get out of this cross tumble we must not carry on, we only want steerage-way to keep her head straight."

Never before had Archie Forbes seen a great gale in all its strength at sea, for those which had occurred while at Rathlin were as nothing to the present; and although on the hillside round Glen Cairn the wind sometimes blew with a force which there was no withstanding, there was nothing to impress the senses as did this wild confusion and turmoil of water. Buoyant as was the boat, heavy seas often broke on board her, and two hands were constantly employed in baling; still Archie judged from the countenance of the men that they did not deem the position desperate, and that they believed the craft would weather the gale. Toward midday, although the wind blew as strongly as ever, there was a sensible change in the motion of the boat. She no longer was tossed up and down with jerky and sudden motion, as the waves seemed to rise directly under her, but rose and fell on the following waves with a steady and regular motion.

"We are well abreast of Islay," the old fisherman said when Archie remarked on the change to him. "There! do you not see that dark bank through the mist; that is Islay. We have no longer a cross sea, and can show a little more sail to keep her from being pooped. We will bear a little off toward the land—we must keep it in sight, and not too far on our left, otherwise we may miss the straits and run on to Jura."

A little more sail was accordingly shown to the gale, and the boat scudded along at increased speed.

"How far is it to Colonsay?" Archie asked.

"Between fifty and sixty miles from Rathlin," the fisherman said. "It was eight o'clock when we started, ten when the squall struck us, it will be dark by four, and fast as we are running we shall scarcely be in time to catch the last gleam of day. Come, boys," he said to his sons, "give her a little more canvas still, for it is life and death to reach Colonsay before nightfall, for if we miss it we shall be dashed on to the Mull long before morning.

A little more sail was accordingly shown, and the boat tore through the water at what seemed to Archie to be tremendous speed; but she was shipping but little water now, for though the great waves as they neared her stern seemed over and over again to Archie as if they would break upon her and send her instantly to the bottom, the stout boat always lifted lightly upon them until he at length felt free from apprehension on that score. Presently the fisherman pointed out a dark mass over their other bow.

"That is Jura," he said; "we are fair for the channel, lads, but you must take in the sail again to the smallest rag, for the wind will blow through the gap between the islands with a force fit to tear the mast out of her."

Through the rest of his life Archie Forbes regarded that passage between Islay and Jura as the most tremendous peril he had ever encountered. Strong as the wind had been before, it was as nothing to the force with which it swept down the strait—the height of the waves was prodigious, and the boat, as it passed over the crest of a wave, seemed to plunge down a very abyss. The old fisherman crouched low in the boat holding the helm, while the other three lay on the planks in the bottom. Speech was impossible, for the loudest shouts would have been drowned in the fury of the storm.   In half an hour the worst was over.   They were through the straits and out in the open sea again, but Islay now made a lee for them, and the sea, high as it was, was yet calm in comparison to the tremendous waves in the Strait of Jura.   More sail was hoisted again, and in an hour the fisherman said, " Thank God, there are the islands."   The day was already fading, and Archie could with difficulty make out the slightly dark mass to which the helm pointed.

"Is that Colonsay?" he asked.

"It is Oronsay," the fisherman said.   " The islands are close together and seem as if they had once been one, but have been cleft asunder by the arm of a giant.   The strait between them is very narrow, and once within it we shall be perfectly sheltered. We must make as close to the point of the island as we can well go, so as not to touch the rocks, and then turn and enter the strait.   If we keep out any distance we shall be blown past the entrance, and then our only remaining chance is to try and run her on to Colonsay, and take the risk of being drowned as she is dashed upon the rocks."

The light had almost faded when they ran along at the end of Oronsay.   Archie shuddered as he saw the waves break upon the rocks and fly high up into the air, and felt how small was the chance of their escape should they be driven on a coast like that.   They were but fifty yards from the point when they came abreast of its extremity; then the fisherman put down the helm and turned her head toward the strait, which opened on their left.

"Down with the sail and mast, lads, and out with your oars; we must row her in."

Not a moment was lost, the sail was lowered, the mast unstepped, and the oars got out, with a speed which showed how urgent was the occasion. Archie, who did not feel confidence in his power to manage her now in such a sea, took his seat by the man on the stroke thwart, and double-banked his oar. Five minutes desperate rowing and they were under shelter of Oronsay, and were rowing more quickly up the narrow strait and toward the shore of Colonsay, where they intended to land. A quarter of an hour more and they stepped ashore.

The old fisherman raised his hat reverently. "Let us thank God and all the saints," he said, "who have preserved us through such great danger. I have been nigh fifty years at sea, and never was cut in so wild a gale."

For a few minutes all stood silent and bareheaded, returning fervent thanks for their escape.

"It is well," the old man said, as they moved inland, "that I have been so far north before; there are but few in Rathlin who have even been north of Islay, but sometimes when fish have been very plentiful in the island, and the boat for Ayr had already gone, I have taken up a boat-load of fish to the good monks of Colonsay, who, although fairly supplied by their own fishermen, were yet always ready to pay a good price for them. Had you been in a boat with one who knew not the waters, assuredly we must have perished, for neither skill nor courage could have availed us. There! do you see that light ahead? That is the priory, and you may be sure of a welcome there."

The priory door was opened at their ring, and the monk who unclosed it, greatly surprised at visitors on such a night, at once bade them enter when he heard that they were fishermen whom the storm had driven to shelter on the island. The fishermen had to lend their aid to the monk to re-close the door, so great was the power of the wind. The monk shot the bolts, saying, " we need expect no further visitors to-night;" and led them into the kitchen, where a huge fire was blazing.

" Quick, Brother Austin," he said to the monk who acted as cook, " warm up a hot drink for these poor souls, for they must assuredly be well-nigh perished with cold, seeing that they have been wet for many hours and exposed to all the violence of this wintry gale."

Archie and his companions were, indeed, stiff with cold and exposure, and could scarce answer the questions which the monks asked them.

" Have patience, brother! have patience!" Brother Austin said. " When their tongues are unfrozen doubtless they will tell you all that you want to know. Only wait, I pray you, till they have drunk this posset which I am preparing."

The monks' curiosity was not, however, destined to be so speedily satisfied, for just as the voyagers were finishing their hot drinks a monk entered with a message that the prior, having heard that some strangers had arrived, would fain welcome and speak with them in his apartment. They rose at once.

"When the prior has done questioning you," Brother Austin said, "return hither at once. I will set about preparing supper for you, for I warrant me you must need food as well as drink. Fear not but, however great your appetite may be, I will have enough to satisfy it ready by the time you return."

"Welcome to Colonsay!" the prior said as the four men entered his apartment; "but stay—I see you are drenched to the skin; and it were poor hospitality, indeed, to keep you standing thus even to assure you of your welcome. Take them," he said to the monk, "to the guest chamber at once, and furnish them with changes of attire. When they are warm and comfortable return with them hither."

In ten minutes Archie and his companions re-entered the prior's room. The prior looked with some astonishment at Archie; for in the previous short interview he had not noticed the difference in their attire, and had supposed them to be four fishermen. The monk, however, had marked the difference; and on inquiry, finding that Archie was a knight, had furnished him with appropriate attire. The good monks kept a wardrobe to suit guests of all ranks, seeing that many visitors came to the holy priory, and that sometimes the wind and waves brought them to shore in such sorry plight that a change of garments was necessary.

"Ah!" the prior said in surprise; "I crave your pardon, sir knight, that I noticed not your rank when you first entered. The light is somewhat dim, and as you stood there together at the doorway I noticed not that you were of superior condition to the others."

"That might well be, holy prior," Archie said, "seeing that we were more like drowned beasts than Christian men. We have had a marvelous escape from the tempest—thanks to God and his saints!—seeing that we were blown off Rathlin, and have run before the gale down past Islay and through the Straits of Jura. Next to the protection of God and his saints, our escape is due to the skill and courage of my brave companions here, who were as cool and calm in the tempest as if they had been sitting by the ingle-fires at home."

"From Rathlin!" the prior said in surprise, "and through the strait 'twixt Islay and Jura! Truly that was a marvelous voyage in such a gale—and as I suppose, in an open boat. But how comes it, sir knight—if I may ask the question without prying into your private affairs—that you, a knight, were at Rathlin? In so wild and lonely an island men of your rank are seldom to be found."

"There are many there now, holy prior, far higher in rank than myself," Archie replied, "seeing that Robert the Bruce, crowned King of Scotland, James Douglas, and others of his nobles and knights, are sheltering there with him from the English bloodhounds."

"The Bruce at Rathlin!" the prior exclaimed in surprise. "The last ship which came hither from the mainland told us that he was a hunted fugitive in Lennox; and we deemed that seeing the MacDougalls of Lorne and all the surrounding chiefs were hostile to him, and the English scattered thickly over all the low country, he must long ere this have fallen into the hands of his enemies."

"Thanks to heaven's protection," Archie said devoutly, "the king with a few followers escaped and safely reached Rathlin!"

"Thou shouldst not speak of heaven's protection," the prior said sternly, "seeing that Bruce has violated the sanctuary of the church, has slain his enemy within her walls, has drawn down upon himself the anathema of the pope, and has been declared excommunicated and accursed."

"The pope, holy father," Archie replied, "although supreme in all holy things, is but little qualified to judge of the matter, seeing that he draws his information from King Edward, under whose protection he lives. The good Bishops of St Andrew's and Glasgow, with the Abbot of Scone, and many other dignitaries of the Scottish church, have condoned his offense, seeing that it was committed in hot blood and without prior intent. The king himself bitterly regrets the deed, which preys sorely upon his mind; but I can answer for it that

Bruce had no thought of meeting Comyn at Dumfries."

"You speak boldly, young sir," the prior said sternly, "for one over whose head scarce two-and-twenty years can have rolled; but enough now. You are storm-staid and wearied; you are the guests of the convent. I will not keep you further now, for you have need of food and sleep. To-morrow I will speak with you again."

So saying, the prior sharply touched a bell which stood on a table near him. The monk re-entered. The prior waved his hand: "Take these guests to the refectory and see that they have all they stand in need of, and that the bedchambers are prepared. In the morning I would speak to them again."

CHAPTER XV.

A MISSION TO IRELAND.

FATHER AUSTIN was as good as his word, and it was long indeed since Archie had sat down to such a meal as that which was spread for him. Hungry as he was, however, he could scarce keep his eyes open to its conclusion, so great was the fatigue of mind and body; and on retiring to the chamber which the monks had prepared for him, he threw himself on a couch and instantly fell asleep. In the morning the gale still blew violently, but with somewhat less fury than on the preceding evening. He joined the monks at their morning meal in the refectory, and after their repast they gathered round him to listen to his news of what was doing in Scotland; for although at ordinary times pilgrims came not unfrequently to visit the holy isle of Colonsay, in the present stormy times men stirred but little from home, and it was seldom that the monks obtained news of what was passing on the mainland. Presently a servitor brought word that the prior would see Archie.

"It was ill talking last night," the prior said, "with a man hungry and worn out; but I gathered

from what you said that you are not only a follower
of Bruce, but that you were with him at that fatal
day at Dumfries when he drew his dagger upon
Comyn in the sanctuary."

"I was there, holy father," Archie replied, "and
can testify that the occurrence was wholly unpre-
meditated; but Bruce had received sufficient provo-
cation from the Comyn to afford him fair reason
for slaying him wheresoever they might meet. But
none can regret more than he does that that place
of meeting was in a sanctuary. The Comyn and
Bruce had made an agreement together whereby the
former relinquished his own claims to the throne of
Scotland on condition that Bruce, on attaining the
throne, would hand over to him all his lordships in
Carrick and Annandale."

"It were a bad bargain," the prior said, "seeing
that Comyn would then be more powerful than his
king."

"So I ventured to tell the Bruce," Archie replied.

"Thou?" the prior said; "you are young,
sir, to be in a position to offer counsel to Robert
Bruce."

"I am young, holy prior," Archie said modestly;
"but the king is good enough to overlook my
youth in consideration of my fidelity to the cause
of Scotland. My name is Archibald Forbes."

"Sir Archibald Forbes!" the prior repeated, rising; "and are you really that loyal and faithful
Scottish knight who fought ever by the side of Wallace, and have almost alone refused ever to bow the

knee to the English? Even to this lonely isle tales
have come of your valor, how you fought side by
side with Wallace, and were, with Sir John
Grahame, his most trusty friend and confidant.
Many of the highest and noblest of Scotland have
for centuries made their way to the shrine of Colonsay, but none more worthy to be our guest. Often
have I longed to see so brave a champion of our
country, little thinking that you would one day
come a storm-driven guest. Truly am I glad to see
you, and I say it even though you may have shared
in the deed at Dumfries, for which I would fain
hope from your words there is fairer excuse to be
made than I had hitherto deemed. I have thought
that the Bishops of St. Andrew's and Glasgow were
wrong in giving their countenance to a man whom
the holy father had condemned—a man whose prior
history gives no ground for faith in his patriotism,
who has taken up arms, now for, now against, the
English, but has ever been ready to make terms
with the oppressor, and to parade as his courtier at
Westminster. In such a man I can have no faith,
and deem that, while he pretends to fight for Scotland, he is in truth but warring for his own aggran-
dizement. But since you, the follower and friend of
the disinterested and intrepid champion of Scotland,
speak for the Bruce, it may be that my judgment
has been too severe upon him."

Archie now related the incident of his journey to
London to urge Bruce to break with Edward and to
head the national movement. He told how, even

before the discovery of his agreement with Comyn, brought about by the treachery of the latter, Bruce had determined definitely to throw in his cause with that of Scotland; how upon that discovery he had fled north, and, happening to meet Comyn at Dumfries, within the limits of the sanctuary, had, in his indignation and ire at his treachery, drawn and slain him. Then he told the tale of what had taken place after the rout of Methven, how bravely Bruce had borne himself, and had ever striven to keep up the hearts of his companions; how cheerfully he had supported the hardships, and how valiantly he had borne himself both at Methven and when attacked by the MacDougalls of Lorne.

"Whatever his past may have been," Archie concluded, "I hold that now the Bruce is as earnest in the cause of Scotland as was even my dear leader Wallace. In strength and in courage he rivals that valiant knight, for though I hold that Wallace was far more than a match for any man of his time, yet Bruce is a worthy second to him, for assuredly no one in Scotland could cross swords with him on equal chances. That he will succeed in his enterprise it were rash to say, for mighty indeed are the odds against him; but if courage, perseverance, and endurance can wrest Scotland from the hands of the English, Robert Bruce will, if he lives, accomplish the task."

"Right glad am I," the prior replied, "to hear what you have told me. Hitherto, owing to my memory of his past and my horror at his crime—

for though from what you tell me there was much
to excuse it, still it was a grievous crime—I have
had but little interest in the struggle, but henceforth
this will be changed. You may tell the king that
from this day, until death or victory crown his
efforts, prayers will be said to heaven night and day
at Colonsay for his success."

It was four days before the storm was over and
the sea sufficiently calmed to admit of Archie's de-
parture. During that time he remained as the honored guest of the priory, and the good monks vied
with the prior in their attentions to the young
knight, the tales of whose doings, as one of Scotland's foremost champions, had so often reached
their lonely island. At the end of that time, the
sea being now calm and smooth, with a light wind
from the north, Archie bade adieu to his hosts and
sailed from Colonsay.

Light as the wind was, it sufficed to fill the sail;
and as the boat glided over the scarce rippled water
Archie could not but contrast the quiet, sleepy
motion with the wild speed at which the boat had
torn through the water on her northern way. It
was not until the following morning that Rathlin
again came in sight.

As the boat was seen approaching, and was
declared by the islanders to be that which they had
regarded as lost in the storm a week previously, the
king, Douglas, and the rest of his followers made
their way down to the shore; and loud was the
shout of welcome which arose when Archie stood
up and waved his hand.

"Verily, Archie Forbes," the king said, as he warmly embraced the young knight, "I shall begin to think that the fairies presided at your birth and gave you some charm to preserve your life alike against the wrath of men and of the elements. Never assuredly did any one pass through so many dangers unscathed as you have done."

"I hope to pass through as many more, sire, in your service," Archie said, smiling.

"I hope so, indeed," Bruce replied; "for it were an evil day for me and for Scotland that saw you fall; but henceforth I will fret no more concerning you. You alone of Wallace's early companions have survived. You got free from Dunstaffnage by some miracle which you have never fully explained to me, and now it would seem that even the sea refuses to swallow you."

"I trust," Archie said more gravely, "that the old saying is not true in my case, and that hanging is not to be my fate. Assuredly it will be if I ever fall into the hands of Edward, and I shall think it a cruel fate indeed if fortune, which has spared me so often in battle, leads me to that cruel end at last."

"I trust not, indeed, Sir Archie," the king said, "though hanging now has ceased to be a dishonorable death when so many of Scotland's best and bravest have suffered it at the English hands. However, I cannot but think that your fairy godmother must have reserved for you the fate of the heroes of most of the stories of my old nurse, which always wound up with 'and so he married, and lived hap-

pily ever after.' And now, Archie, tell me all that
has befallen you, where you have been, and how
you have fared, and by what miraculous chance you
escaped the tempest. All our eyes were fixed on
the boat when you labored to reach the shore, and
had you heard the groans we uttered when we saw
you give up the effort as hopeless and fly away to
sea before the wind you would have known how
truly all your comrades love you. We gave you up
as assuredly lost, for the islanders here agreed that
you had no chance of weathering the gale, and that
the boat would, ere many hours, be dashed to pieces
either on Islay or Jura, should it even reach so far ;
but the most thought that you would founder long
ere you came in sight of the land."

Accompanying the king with his principal companions to the hut which he occupied, Archie related
the incidents of the voyage and of their final refuge
at Colonsay.

"It was a wonderful escape," the king said when
he finished, "and the holy Virgin and the saints
must assuredly have had you in their especial care.
You have cost us well nigh a fortune, for not one
of us but vowed offerings for your safety, which
were, perchance, the more liberal, since we deemed
the chances of paying them so small. However,
they shall be redeemed, for assuredly they have
been well earned, and for my share I am bound,
when I come to my own, to give a piece of land of
the value of one hundred marks a year to the good
monks of St. Killians to be spent in masses for the
souls of those drowned at sea."

Some days later the king said to Archie, " I have a mission for you; 'tis one of danger, but I know that that is no drawback in your eyes."

" I am ready," Archie said modestly, " to carry out to the best of my power any errand with which your majesty may intrust me."

" I have been thinking, Sir Archie, that I might well make some sort of alliance with the Irish chieftains. Many of these are, like most of our Scotch nobles, on terms of friendship with England; still there are others who hold aloof from the conquerors. It would be well to open negotiations with these, so that they by rising might distract Edward's attention from Scotland, while we, by our efforts, would hinder the English from sending all their force thither, and we might thus mutually be of aid to each other. At present I am, certes, in no position to promise aid in men or money; but I will bind myself by an oath that if my affairs in Scotland prosper I will from my treasury furnish money to aid them in carrying on the struggle, and that if I clear Scotland of her oppressors I will either go myself or send one of my brothers with a strong force to aid the Irish to follow our example. The mission is, as you will see, Sir Archie, a dangerous one; for should any of the English, or their Irish allies, lay hands on you, your doom would be sealed. Still you may do me and Scotland great service should you succeed in your mission. Even minor risings would be of much utility, seeing that they would at any rate prevent Edward from bringing over troops from Ireland to assist in our conquest. I have thought the matter over deeply, and conclude that, young as you are, I can intrust it to you with confidence, and that you are indeed the best fitted among those with me to undertake it. Douglas is but a boy; my brother Edward is too hot and rash; Boyd is impatient and headstrong, trusty and devoted to me though he is; but I am sure that in you there is no lack either of prudence or courage. Hence, Sir Archie, if you will undertake it I will intrust it to you."

"I will willingly undertake it, sire, since you think me fitting for it, and deem it a high honor indeed that you have chosen me. When will you that I start?"

"It were best to lose no time," the king replied, "and if you have no reason for delay I would that you should embark to-night, so that before daybreak you may have gained the Irish shore. They tell me that there are many desperate men in refuge among the caves on the coast, and among these you might choose a few who might be useful to you in your project; but it is not in this part that a rising can be effected, for the country inland is comparatively flat and wholly in the hands of the English. It is on the west coast that the resistance to the English was continued to the last, and here from time to time it blazes out again. In those parts, as they tell me, not only are there wild mountains and fastnesses such as we have in Scotland, but there are great morasses and swamps, extending over wide tracts, where heavy-armed soldiers cannot penetrate, and where many people still maintain a sort of wild independence, defying all the efforts of the English to subdue them. The people are wild and savage, and ever ready to rise against the English. Here, then, is the country where you are most likely to find chiefs who may enter into our plans, and agree to second our efforts for independence. Here are some rings and gold chains, which are all that remain to me of my possessions. Money I have none; but with these you may succeed in winning the hearts of some of these savage chieftains. Take, too, my royal signet, which will be a guarantee that you have power to treat in my name. I need not tell you to be brave, Sir Archie; but be prudent—remember that your life is of the utmost value to me. I want you not to fight, but simply to act as my envoy. If you succeed in raising a great fire in the west of Ireland, remain there and act as councillor to the chiefs, remembering that you are just as much fighting for Scotland there as if you were drawing sword against her foes at home. If you find that the English arm is too strong, and the people too cowed and disheartened to rise against it, then make your way back here by the end of three months, by which time I hope to sail hence and to raise my standard in Scotland again."

On leaving the king Archie at once conferred with Duncan the fisherman, who willingly agreed that night to set him ashore in Ireland.

"I will land you," he said, "at a place where you
need not fear that any English will meet you.
It is true that they have a castle but three miles
away perched on a rock on the coast. It is called
Dunluce, and commands a wide seaward view, and
for this reason it were well that our boat were far
out at sea again before morning dawned, so that if
they mark us they will not suppose that we have
touched on the coast; else they might send a party
to search if any have landed—not even then that
you need fear discovery, for the coast abounds in
caves and hiding-places. My sons have often
landed there, for we do a certain trade in the
summer from the island in fish and other matters
with the natives there. If it please you, my son
Ronald, who is hardy and intelligent, shall land
with you and accompany you as your retainer while
you remain in Ireland. The people there speak a
language quite different to that which you use in
the lowlands of Scotland and in England, but the
language we speak among ourselves closely resembles it, and we can be easily understood by the
people of the mainland. You would be lost did you
go among the native Irish without an interpreter."

Archie thankfully accepted the offer, and that
night, after bidding adieu to the friends and his
comrades, started in Duncan's boat.

"'Tis a strange place where I am going to land
you," the fisherman said; "such a place as nowhere
else have my eyes beheld, though they say that at
the Isle of Staffa, far north of Colonsay, a similar

sight is to be seen. The rocks, instead of being rugged or square, rise in close columns like the trunks of trees, or like the columns in the church of the priory of Colonsay. Truly they seem as if wrought by the hands of men, or rather of giants, seeing that no men could carry out so vast a work. The natives have legends that they are the work of giants of old times. How this may be I know not, though why giants should have engaged in so useless a work passes my understanding. However, there are the pillars, whosoever placed them there. Some of them are down by the level of the sea. Here their heads seem to be cut off so as to form a landing-place, to which the natives give the name of the Giant's Causeway. Others in low rows stand on the face of the cliff itself, though how any could have stood there to work them, seeing that no human foot can reach the base, is more than I can say. 'Tis a strange and wonderful sight, as you will say when the morning light suffers you to see it."

It was fortunate that Duncan knew the coast so well, and was able by the light of the stars to find a landing-place, for quiet as the sea appeared a swell rose as they neared the shore, and the waves beat heavily on the wild and rocky coast. Duncan, however, steered his boat to the very foot of the causeway, and then, watching his opportunity, Archie sprang ashore followed by Ronald. A few words of adieu were spoken, and then the boat rowed out to sea again, while Archie and Ronald turned away from the landing-place.

"It were best," the young fisherman said, "to find a seat among the rocks, and there to await the dawn, when I can guide you to some caves hard by; but in the darkness we might well fall and break a limb did we try and make our way across the coast."

A niche was soon found, and Archie and his companion sat down for awhile. Archie, however, soon discovered that the sides and back of his seat were formed of the strange columns of which Duncan had spoken, and that he was sitting upon the tops of others which had broken off. Eagerly he passed his hands over the surface of these strange pillars and questioned his companion as to what he knew about them; but Ronald could tell him no more than his father had done, and Archie was forced to await the dawn to examine more closely the strange columns. Daylight only added to his wonder. On all sides of him stretched the columns packed in a dense mass together, while range above range they stood on the face of the great cliffs above him. The more he examined them, the more his wonder grew.

"They can neither be the work of men nor giants," he said, "but must have been called up by the fantastic freak of some powerful enchanter. Hitherto I have not believed the tales of these mysterious beings of old times; but after seeing these wonderful pillars I can no longer doubt, for assuredly no mortal hand could have done this work."

Ronald now urged that they had better be moving

as it was possible, although unlikely enough, that one passing along the top of the cliffs might get sight of them. They accordingly moved along the shore, and in a quarter of a mile reached the mouth of a great cave. The bottom was covered with rocks, which had fallen from the roof, thickly clustered over with wet seaweed, which, indeed, hung from the sides far up, showing that at high tide the sea penetrated far into the cave.

"The ground rises beyond," Ronald said, "and you will find recessses there which the tide never reaches." They moved slowly at first until their eyes became accustomed to the darkness; then they kept on, the ground getting more even as they ascended, until they stood on a dry and level floor.

"Now I will strike a light," Ronald said, "and light the torch which I brought with me. We are sure to find plenty of driftwood cast up at the highest point the tide reaches. Then we can make a fire, and while you remain here I will go out and find some of the natives, and engage a guide to take us forward to-night."

Taking out his flint and steel, Ronald proceeded to strike a light, and after several efforts succeeded in doing so and in igniting some dried moss which he had brought with him, carefully shielded from damp in the folds of his garment. As a light flame rose he applied his torch to it; but as he did so, came an exclamation of astonishment, for gathered in a circle round them were a dozen wild figures. All were armed and stood in readiness to strike down the intruders into their hiding-place. They were barefooted, and had doubtless been asleep in the cave until, when awakened by the approaching footsteps and voices, they had silently arisen and prepared to fall upon the intruders.

"We are friends," Ronald said in the native language when he recovered from his first start of surprise. "I am Ronald, a fisherman from Rathlin, and was over here in the summer exchanging fish for sheep."

"I recollect you," one of the men said; "but what do you here so strangely and secretly? Are the English hunting you too from your island as they have done us?"

"They have not come to Rathlin yet," Ronald said. "Doubtless they would do so, but 'tis too poor to offer any temptation for their greed. But they are our enemies as they are yours. I am here to guide this Scottish knight, who is staying at Rathlin, a fugitive from their vengeance like yourself, and who is charged with a mission from the King of Scotland to your chiefs, whom he would fain induce to join in a rising against the power of the English."

"He is welcome," the man who appeared to be the leader of the party replied, "and may he succeed in his object; but," he continued bitterly, "I fear that the chance is a small one. The Norman foot is on our necks, and most of those who should be our leaders have basely accepted the position of vassals to the English king. Still there are brave hearts yet in Ireland who would gladly rise did they see even a faint chance of success. Hundreds are there who, like us, prefer to live the lives of hunted dogs in caves, in mountain fastnesses, or in the bogs, rather than yield to the English yoke. Tell me your plans and whither you would go; and I will give you guides who know every foot of the country, and who can lead you to the western hills, where, though no open resistance is made, the English have scarce set foot. There we generally find refuge; and 'tis only at times, when the longing to see the homes of our childhood becomes too strong for us, that I and these you see—all of whom were born and reared between this and Coleraine—come hither for a time, when at night we can issue out and prowl round the ruins of the homes of our fathers."

While this conversation had been going on, the others, seeing that the visit was a friendly one, had set to work, and bringing up driftwood from below, piled it round the little blaze which Ronald had commenced, and soon had a great fire lighted. They then produced the carcass of a sheep which they had the evening before carried off. Ronald had brought with him a large pile of oaten-cakes, and a meal was speedily prepared.

Archie could not but look with surprise at the wild figures around him, lit up by the dancing glare of the fire. Their hair lay in tangled masses on their necks; their attire was of the most primitive description, consisting but of one garment secured round the waist by a strap of untanned leather; their feet and legs were bare. Their hair was almost black; their eyes small and glittering, with heavy overhanging brows; and they differed altogether in appearance even from the wildest and poorest of the Scottish peasantry. In their belts all bore long knives of rough manufacture, and most of them carried slings hanging from the belt, in readiness for instant use. In spite of the wildness of their demeanor they seemed kindly and hospitable; and many were the questions which they asked Ronald concerning the King of Scotland and his knights who were in refuge at Rathlin.

When the meal was over all stretched themselves on the sand like so many animals, and without further preparation went off to sleep. Archie, knowing that nothing could be done until nightfall, followed their example. The fire had by this time burned low, and soon perfect stillness reigned in the great cavern, save that far away at its mouth the low thunder of the waves upon the rocks came up in a confused roar.

CHAPTER XVI.

AN IRISH RISING.

WHEN night came on Archie started for the west,
accompanied by Ronald and two of the Irish as
guides. They crossed the country without question
or interference, and reached the wild mountains of
Donegal in safety. Archie had asked that his con-
ductors should lead him to the abode of the principal chieftain of the district. The miserable appearance of the sparsely scattered villages through
which they had passed had prepared him to find
that the superiors of such a people would be in a
very different position from the feudal lords of the
highlands of Scotland. He was not surprised, therefore, when his attendants pointed out a small hold,
such as would appertain to a small landowner on the
Scottish border, as the residence of the chief.
Around it were scattered a number of low huts
composed of turf, roofed with reeds. From these,
when the approach of strangers was reported, a
number of wild-looking figures poured out, armed
with weapons of the most primitive description. A
shout from Archie's guides assured these people
that the newcomer was not, as his appearance

betokened him, a Norman knight, but a visitor from Scotland who sought a friendly interview with the chief.

Insignificant as was the hold, it was evident that something like feudal discipline was kept up. Two men, armed with pikes, were stationed on the wall, while two others leaned in careless fashion against the posts of the open gate. On the approach of Archie an elderly man, with a long white beard, came out to meet them. Ronald explained to him that Archie was a knight who had come as an emissary from the King of Scotland to the Irish chieftains, and desired to speak with the great Fergus of Killeen. The old man bowed deeply to Archie, and then escorted him into the house.

The room which they entered occupied the whole of the ground-floor of the hold, and was some thirty feet wide by forty long. As apparently trees of sufficient length to form the beams of so wide an apartment could not be obtained, the floor above was supported by two rows of roughly-squared posts extending down from end to end. The walls were perfectly bare. The beams and planks of the ceiling were stained black by the smoke of a fire which burned in one corner; the floor was of clay beaten hard. A strip some ten feet wide, at the further end, was raised eighteen inches above the general level, forming a sort of dais. Here, in a carved settle of black wood, sat the chief. Some females, evidently the ladies of his family, were seated on piles of sheepskins, and were plying their distaffs;

while an aged man was seated on the end of the
dais with a harp of quaint form on his knee; his
fingers touched a last chord as Archie entered, and
he had evidently been playing while the ladies
worked. Near him on the dais was a fire composed
of wood embers, which were replenished from time
to time with fresh glowing pieces of charcoal taken
from the fire at the other end of the room, so that
the occupants of the dais should not be annoyed by
the smoke arising close to them.

The chief was a fine-looking man about fifty years
old. He was clad in a loose-fitting tunic of soft
dark-green cloth, confined at the waist by a broad
leathern band with silver clasp and ornaments, and
reaching to his knees. His arms were bare; on his
feet he wore sandals, and a heavy sword rested
against the wall near his hand. The ladies wore
dresses of similar material and of somewhat similar
fashion, but reaching to the feet. They wore gold
armlets; and the chief's wife had a light band of
gold round her head. The chief rose when Archie
entered; and upon the seneschal informing him of
the rank and mission of his visitor he stepped from
the dais, and advancing, greeted him warmly. Then
he led him back to the dais, where he presented to
him the ladies of his family, ordering the retainers,
of whom about a score were gathered in the hall, to
place two piles of sheepskins near the fire. On one
of these he sat down, and motioned to Archie to take
his place on the other—his own chair being removed
to a corner. Then, through the medium of Ronald,
the conversation began.

Archie related to the chief the efforts which the
Scotch were making to win their freedom from England, and urged in the king's name that a similar
effort should be made by the Irish; as the forces of
the English, being thereby divided and distracted,
there might be better hope of success. The chief
heard the communication in grave silence. The ladies
of the family stood behind the chief with deeply-
interested faces; and as the narrative of the long-
continued struggle which the Scots were making for
freedom continued it was clear, by their glowing
cheeks and their animated faces, how deeply they
sympathized in the struggle.

The wife of the chief, a tall and stately lady, stood
immediately behind him with her two daughters,
girls of some seventeen or eighteen years of age,
beside her. As Ronald was translating his words
Archie glanced frequently at the group, and thought
he had never seen one fairer or more picturesque.
There was a striking likeness between mother and
daughters; but the expression of staid dignity in
the one was in the others replaced by a bright
expression of youth and happiness. Their beauty
was of a kind new to Archie. Their dark glossy
hair was kept smoothly in place by the fillet of gold
in the mother's case, and by purple ribbons in that
of the daughters. Their eyebrows and long eye-
lashes were black, but their eyes were gray, and as
light as those to which Archie was accustomed
under the fair tresses of his countrywomen. The
thing that struck him most in the faces of the girls

was their mobility, the expression changing as it seemed in an instant from grave to gay—flushing at one moment with interest at the tale of deeds of valor, paling at the next at the recital of cruel oppression and wrong. When Archie had finished his narrative he presented to the chief a beautifully wrought chain of gold as a token from the King of Scotland. The chief was silent for some time after the interpreter concluded Archie's narrative; then he said:

"Sir knight, it almost seems to me as if I had been listening to the tale of the wrongs of Ireland, save that it appears that the mastery of the English here has been more firmly established than with you. This may be from the nature of the country; our hills are, for the most part, bare, while yours, you say, are covered with forest. Thus the Normans could more easily, when they had once gained the upper hand, crush out the last vestiges of opposition than they could with you. As I judge from what you say, the English in Scotland hold all the fortresses, and when the people rise they remain sheltered in them until assistance comes from England. With us it is different. First they conquer all the country; then from a wide tract, a third perhaps of the island, they drive out the whole of the people, and establish themselves firmly there, portioning the land among the soldiery and repeopling the country with an English race. Outside this district the Irish chieftains, like myself, retain something of independence; we pay a tribute, and

are in the position of feudatories, being bound to
furnish so many men for the King of England's
wars if called upon to do so. The English seldom
come beyond their pale so long as the tribute is
paid, and the yoke, therefore, weighs not so heavy
upon us; but were we to rise, the English army
would pour out from its pale and carry fire and
sword throughout the country.

"We, like you, have been without one who would
unite us against the common enemy. Our great
chiefs have, for the most part, accepted English
titles, and since their power over the minor chiefs
is extended, rather than decreased by the changed
circumstances, they are well content, for they
rule now over their districts, not only as Irish
chieftains, but as English lieutenants. You have
seen, as you journeyed here, how sparse is the
population of our hills, and how slight would be
the opposition which we could offer, did the Earl
of Ulster sweep down upon us with trained English
soldiers.

"Were there a chance of success, Fergus of Killeen would gladly draw the sword again; but I will
not bring ruin upon my family and people by
engaging in a hopeless enterprise. Did I raise my
standard, all Donegal would take up arms; but
Donegal alone is powerless against England. I
know my people—they are ready for the fray, they
would rush to battle and perish in thousands to
win victory, but one great defeat would crush them.
The story of the long fight which your Wallace,

with a small following, made against the power of England, will never be told of an Irish leader. We have bravery and reckless courage, but we have none of the stubborn obstinacy of your Scottish folk. Were the flag raised the people would flock to it, and would fight desperately; but if they lost, there would be utter and complete collapse. The fortitude to support repeated defeats, to struggle on when the prospect seems darkest, does not belong to my people.

"It is for this reason that I have no hope that Ireland will ever regain its independence. She may struggle against the yoke, she may blaze out again and again in bloody risings, our sons may die in tens of thousands for her; but never, I believe, as long as the men of the two countries remain what they are, will Ireland recover her independence, for, in the long run, English perseverance and determination will overcome the fitful courage of the Irish. I grieve that I should say it. I mourn that I feel it my duty to repress rather than to encourage the eager desire of my people to draw the sword and strike for feedom; but such is my conviction.

"But understand, sir knight, that whatever I may think, I shall not be backward in doing my part. If Ireland again rises, should the other native chieftains determine to make one more effort to drive the English across the channel, be sure that Fergus of Killeen and the men of Donegal will be in the front of the battle. No heart beats more warmly for freedom than mine; and did I stand alone I would take to the bogs and join those who shelter there, defying the might of England. But I have my people to think of. I have seen how the English turn a land to desolation as they sweep across it, and I will not bring fire and sword into these mountain valleys unless all Ireland is banded in a common effort. You have seen Scotland wasted from sea to sea, her cities burned, her people slain by thousands, her dales and valleys wasted; and can you tell me that after these years of struggle you have gained any such advantage as would warrant your advising me to rise against England?"

Archie was silent. Thinking over the struggle in which he had taken part for so many years, and remembering the woes that it had brought on Scotland, and that, after fighting so long, Bruce and the handful of fugitives at Rathlin were the sole survivors of the patriotic party, he could not but acknowledge at heart the justice of the chief's words. His sole hope for Scotland now rested in the perseverance and personal valor of the king, and the stubborn character of the people, which he felt assured would lead them to rise again and again, in spite of disaster and defeat, until freedom was won. The Irish possessed no Bruce; their country was less defendible than Scotland; and if, as Fergus said, they had none of that indomitable perseverance which enabled the Scotch people again and again to rise against the yoke, what hope

could there be of final success, how could he be
justified in urging upon the chieftain a step which
would bring fire and sword into those quiet valleys!
For some time, therefore, after Ronald had translated the chief's speech he remained silent.

"I will not urge you further, sir," he said, "for
you are surely the best judge of what is good for
your people, and I have seen such ruin and desolation in Scotland, so many scores of ruined towns
and villages, so many thousands of leveled home-
steads, that I will not say a single word to urge you
to alter your resolution. It is enough for me that
you have said that if Ireland rises you will also
draw the sword. I must carry out my instructions,
and hence shall travel south and visit other chiefs ;
they may view matters differently, and may see
that what Ireland cannot do alone she may do in
conjunction with Scotland."

"So be it!" Fergus said. "Believe me, if you
raise a flame through the west the north will not
hang back. And now I trust that you will remain
here for a few days as my guest. All that I
have is yours, and my wife and daughters will do
their best to make the time pass pleasantly for
you."

Archie remained three days at the chief's hold,
where the primitive life interested him greatly. A
lavish hospitality was exercised. Several sheep were
killed and roasted each day, and all comers were free
to join the repast. The chief's more immediate retainers, some twenty in number, ate, lived, and slept

'n the great hall; while tables were spread outside,
at which all who came sat down without question.
The upper rooms of the hold were occupied by the
chief, the ladies of his family, and the female domes-
tics. Here they retired when they felt disposed, but
their meals were served on the dais. In the evening the harper played and sang legends of deeds of
bravery in the day of Ireland's independence; and
as Ronald translated the songs to him Archie could
not but conclude privately that civil war, rapine,
strife, and massacre must have characterized the
country in those days.

At the conclusion of his stay Fergus appointed
two of the retainers to accompany Archie south,
and to give assurance to the various wild people
through whom he might pass, that Archie's mission was a friendly one to Ireland, and that he
was an honored friend and guest of the chief of
Killeen.

On his arrival in Mayo Archie found matters
more favorable to his mission. An insurrection had
already broken out, headed by some of the local
chieftains, originating in a broil between the English soldiers of a garrison and the natives. The
garrison had been surprised and massacred, and the
wild Irish were flocking to arms. By the chieftains
here Archie, on explaining his mission, was warmly
welcomed. As they were already in arms no urging
on his part was needed, and they despatched messengers throughout the country, saying that an emissary from Scotland had arrived, and calling upon all

to rise and to join with the Scotch in shaking off the yoke of England.

Archie had therefore to travel no further, and decided that he could best carry out his mission by assisting to organize and lead the Irish forces. These he speedily discovered were beyond all comparison inferior, both in arms, in discipline, and in methods of fighting, to the Scots. For a dashing foray they would be excellent. Hardy, agile, and full of impetuosity, they would bear down all resistance instantly, were that resistance not too strong; but against stubborn and well-armed troops they would break like a wave against a rock. Archie saw that with such troops anything like regular war would be impossible, and that the struggle must be one of constant surprises, attacks, and forays, and that they could succeed only by wearing out and not by defeating the enemy. With such tactics as these they might by long perseverance succeed; but this was just what Fergus had warned him they would not practice, and that their courage was rather of a kind which would lead them to dash desperately against the line of leveled spears, rather than continue a long and weary struggle under apparently hopeless circumstances.

The chiefs, hearing from Archie that he had acted as one of Wallace's lieutenants in battles where the English had been heavily defeated, willingly consented that he should endeavor to instil the tactics by which those battles had been won into their own followers; but when they found that he proposed that the men should remain stationary to withstand the English charges, they shook their heads.

"That will never do for our people," they said. "They must attack sword in hand. They will rush fearlessly down against any odds, but you will never get them steadily to withstand a charge of men-at-arms."

Archie, however, persuaded them to allow him to organize a band of two hundred men under his immediate orders. These were armed with long pikes, and were to form a sort of reserve, in order that if the wild charge of the main body failed in its object these could cover a retreat, or serve as a nucleus around which they could rally. The army swelled rapidly; every day fresh chiefs arrived with scores of wild tribesmen. Presently the news came that an English force was advancing from the pale against them.

A council was held at which Archie was present. Very strongly he urged his views upon the chieftains, namely: that they should altogether decline a pitched battle; but that, divided into numerous parties, they should enter the pale, destroying weak garrisons and ravaging the country, trying to wear out the English by constant skirmishes and night attacks, but refusing always to allow themselves to be tempted into an engagement.

"The English cannot be everywhere at once," he urged. "Let them hold only the ground on which their feet stand. As they advance or retire, close ever in on their rear, drive off their cattle and destroy their crops and granaries in the pale ; force them to live wholly in their walled towns, and as you gain in strength capture these one by one, as we did in Scotland. So, and so only, can you hope for ultimate success."

His advice was received with a silence which he at once saw betokened disapproval. One after another of the Irish chieftains rose and declared that such a war could not be sustained.

"Our retainers," they said, "are ready to fight, but after fighting they will want to return to their homes ; besides, we are fifteen thousand strong, and the English men-at-arms marching against us are but eight hundred ; it would be shameful and cowardly to avoid a battle, and were we willing to do so our followers would not obey us. Let us first destroy this body of English, then we shall be joined by others, and can soon march straight upon Dublin."

Archie saw that it was hopeless to persevere, and set out the following day with the wild rabble, for they could not be termed an army, to meet the English. The leaders yielded so far to his advice as to take up a position where they would fight with the best chance of success. The spot lay between a swamp extending a vast distance, and a river, and they were thus open only to an attack in front, and could, if defeated, take refuge in the bog, where horsemen could not follow them.

On the following morning the English were seen

approaching. In addition to the eight hundred men-at-arms were one thousand lightly-equipped footmen, for experience had taught the English commanders that in such a country lightly-armed men were necessary to operate where the wide extending morasses prevented the employment of cavalry. The English advanced in solid array: three hundred archers led the way; these were followed by seven hundred spearmen, and the men-at-arms brought up the rear. The Irish were formed in disordered masses, each under its own chieftain. The English archers commenced the fight with a shower of arrows. Scarcely had these begun to fall when the Irish with a tremendous yell rushed forward to the assault. The English archers were swept like chaff before them. With reckless bravery they threw themselves next upon the spearmen. The solid array was broken by the onslaught, and in a moment both parties were mixed up in wild confusion.

The sight was too much for Archie's band to view unmoved, and these, in spite of his shouts, left their ground and rushed at full speed after their companions and threw themselves into the fight.

Archie was mounted, having been presented with a horse by one of the chiefs, and he now, although hopeless of the final result, rode forward. Just as he joined the confused and struggling mass the English men-at-arms burst down upon them. As a torrent would cleave its way through a mass of loose sand, so the English men-at-arms burst through the mass of Irish, trampling and cutting down all in their path. Not unharmed, however, for the Irish fought desperately with axe and knife, hewing at the men-at-arms, stabbing at the horses, and even trying by sheer strength to throw the riders to the ground. After passing through the mass the men at-arms turned and again burst down upon them. It was a repetition of the first charge. The Irish fought desperately, but it was each for himself; there was neither order nor cohesion, and each man strove only to kill a foe before being himself slain. Archie and the chiefs with the few mounted men among the retainers, strove in vain to stem the torrent. Under the orders of their leaders the English kept in a compact mass, and the weight of the horses and armor bore down all opposition. Four times did the men-at-arms burst through the struggling mass of Irish. As they formed to charge the fifth time the latter lost heart, and as if acting under a simultaneous influence they turned and fled.

The English horse burst down on the rear of the mass of fugitives, hewing them down in hundreds. Those nearest to the river dashed in, and numbers were drowned in striving to cross it. The main body, however, made for the swamp, and though in the crush many sank in and perished miserably here, the grea t majority, leaping lightly from tuft to tuft, gained the heart of the morass, the pursuing horse reining up on its edge.

Ronald had kept near Archie in the fight, and when all was lost ran along by the side of his horse, holding fast to the stirrup leather. The horsemen still pressed along between the river and the morass, and Archie, following the example of several of the chiefs, alighted from his saddle, and with his companion entered the swamp. It was with the greatest difficulty that he made his way across it, and his lightly-armed companion did him good service in assisting several times to drag him from the treacherous mire when he began to sink in it. At last they reached firmer ground in the heart of the swamp, and here some five thousand or six thousand fugitives were gathered. At least four thousand had fallen on the field. Many had escaped across the river, although numbers had lost their lives in the attempt. Others scattered and fled in various directions. A few of the chiefs were gathered in council when Archie arrived. They agreed that all was lost and there was nothing to do but to scatter to their homes. Archie took no part in the discussion. That day's experience had convinced him that nothing like a permanent and determined insurrection was possible, and only by such a movement could the Scottish cause be aided, by forcing the English to send reinforcements across St. George's Channel. After seeing the slaughter which had taken place, he was rejoiced at heart that the rising had commenced before he joined it, and was in no way the result of his mission, but was one of the sporadic insurrections which frequently broke out in Ireland, only to be instantly and sternly repressed.

"We have failed, sir knight," one of the chiefs said to him, "but it was not for want of courage on the part of our men."

"No, indeed," Archie replied through his interpreter; "never did I see men fight more fiercely, but without discipline and organization victory is well-nigh impossible for lightly-armed footmen against heavy mail-clad cavalry."

"The tactics you advised were doubtless good," the chief said; "I see their wisdom, but they are well-nigh impossible to carry out with such following as ours. They are ever impatient for the fray, but quickly wearied by effort; ready to die, but not to wait; to them prudence means cowardice, and their only idea of fighting is to rush full at a foe. See how they broke the English spearmen!"

"It was right well done," Archie replied, "and some day, when well trained and disciplined, Irish soldiers will be second to none in the world; but unless they will submit to training and discipline they can never hope to conquer the English."

"And now, sir knight, what do you propose doing?" the chief said.

"I shall make my way north," Archie replied, "and shall rejoin my king at Rathlin."

"I will send two of my men with you. They know every foot of the morasses of this neighborhood, and when they get beyond the point familiar to them will procure you two others to take their places. It will need all your prudence and courage to get through, for the English men-at-arms will be

scouring the country in groups of four, hunting all
those they come across like wolves. See, already !"
and he pointed to the horizon; " they are scattering round the edge of the morass to inclose us
here; but it is many miles round, and before to-
morrow is gone not a man will be left here."

When darkness fell, Archie, accompanied by
Ronald and his guides, set out on his journey.
Alone he could never have found his way through
the swamps, but even in the darkness his guides
moved along quickly, following tracks known to
them with the instinct of hounds; Archie kept
close on their heels, as a step only a few inches
from the track might plunge him in a deep morass,
in which in a few seconds he would sink out of sight.
On nearing the edge of the bog the guides slackened
their pace. Motioning to Archie to remain where
he was, they crept forward noiselessly into the
darkness. Not far off he could hear the calls of
the English horsemen. The sounds were repeated
again and again until they died away in the distance, showing that a cordon had been drawn round
the morass so as to inclose the fugitives from the
battle of the previous day.

In a quarter of an hour the guides returned as
noiselessly as they had departed, and Archie continued the march at their heels. Even greater
caution than before was now necessary in walking,
for the English, before darkness had set in, had
narrowly examined the edge of the morass, and had
placed three or four men wherever they could dis-

cover the slightest signs of a track. Thus Archie's
guides were obliged to leave the path by which
they had previously traveled. Their progress was
slow now, the party only moving for a few yards at
a time, and then halting while the guides searched
for ground solid enough to carry their weight. At
last Archie felt the ground grow firmer under his
foot, and a reconnoissance by the guides having
shown them that none of the English were stationed
opposite to them, they left the morass, and noiselessly made their way across the country until far
beyond the English line.

All night they walked, and at daybreak entered
another swamp, and lay down for the day in the
long coarse grass growing on a piece of firm ground
deep in its recesses. In the evening one of the
guides stole out and returned with a native of the
neighborhood, who undertook to show Archie the
way on his further journey.

Ten days, or rather nights, of steady journeying
brought Archie again to the rocky shore where he
had landed. Throughout he had found faithful
guides, whom he had rewarded by giving, as was
often the custom of the time, in lieu of money, a
link or two of one of his gold chains. He and
Ronald again took refuge in the cave where they
had passed the first night of their landing. It was
untenanted now.

Here they abode for a fortnight, Ronald going
up every two or three days to purchase provisions
at the scattered cottages. On Saturday night they

lit a great fire just inside the mouth of the cave, so that while the flame could be seen far out at sea the light would be unobserved by the garrison of Dunluce or any straggler on the cliff above. It had been arranged with Duncan that every Saturday night, weather permitting, he should sail across and look for a signal fire. The first Saturday night was wild and stormy, and although they lit the fire they had but slight idea that Duncan would put out. The following week, however, the night was calm and bright, and after piling up the fire high they proceeded to the causeway, and two hours later saw to their joy a boat approaching. In a few minutes they were on board, and by the following morning reached Rathlin.

The king and his companions welcomed Archie's return warmly, although the report which he made showed that there was no hope of obtaining any serious diversion of the English attack by a permanent rising in Ireland ; and the king, on hearing Archie's account of all that had passed, assured him that he felt that, although he had failed, no one, under the circumstances, could have done otherwise.

CHAPTER XVII.

THE KING'S BLOODHOUND.

THE only other event which occurred throughout the winter was the arrival of a fishing-boat with a messenger from one of the king's adherents, and the news which he brought filled them with sorrow and dismay. Kildrummy had been threatened with a siege, and the queen, Bruce's sisters Christine and Mary, his daughter Marjory, and the other ladies accompanying them, deemed it prudent to leave the castle and take refuge in the sanctuary of St. Duthoc, in Ross-shire.

The sanctuary was violated by the Earl of Ross and his followers, and the ladies and their escort delivered up to Edward's lieutenants and sent to England. The knights and squires who formed the escort were all executed, and the ladies committed to various places of confinement, where most of them remained in captivity of the strictest and most rigorous kind until after the battle of Bannockburn, eight years later. The Countess of Buchan, who had crowned Bruce at Scone, and who was one of the party captured at St. Duthoc, received even fouler treatment, by Edward's especial orders, being

placed in a cage on one of the turrets of Berwick
Castle so constructed that she could be seen by all
who passed ; and in this cruel imprisonment she was
kept like a wild beast for seven long years by a
Christian king whom his admirers love to hold up
as a model of chivalry.

Kildrummy had been besieged and taken by
treachery. The king's brother, Nigel Bruce, was
carried to Berwick, and was there hanged and
beheaded. Christopher Seaton and his brother
Alexander, the Earl of Athol, Sir Simon Fraser, Sir
Herbert de Moreham, Sir David Inchmartin, Sir
John Somerville, Sir Walter Logan, and many other
Scotchmen of noble degree, had also been captured
and executed, their only offense being that they
had fought for their country.

In all the annals of England there is no more
disgraceful page than that which chronicles the
savage ferocity with which King Edward behaved
to the Scottish nobles and ladies who fell into his
hands. The news of these murders excited the
utmost fury as well as grief among the party at
Rathlin, and only increased their determination to
fight till the death against the power of England.

The spring was now at hand, and Douglas, with
Archie Forbes and a few followers, left in a boat,
and landed on the Isle of Arran. In the bay of
Brodick was a castle occupied by Sir John Hastings
and an English garrison. The Scots concealed
themselves near the castle, awaiting an opportunity
for an attack. A day or two after their arrival

several vessels arrived with provisions and arms for the garrison. As these were being landed Douglas and his followers sallied out and captured the vessels and stores. The garrison of the castle made a sortie to assist their friends, but were driven in with slaughter, and the whole of the supplies remained in the hands of the Scots, causing great rejoicing to the king and the rest of the party when a few days later they arrived from Rathlin.

Bruce now proposed an immediate descent upon Carrick, there, in the midst of his family possessions, to set up his banner in Scotland. The lands had been forfeited by Edward and bestowed upon some of his own nobles. Annandale had been given to the Earl of Hereford, Carrick to Earl Percy, Selkirk to Aylmer de Valence. The castle of Turnberry was occupied by Percy with three hundred men. Bruce sent on his cousin Cuthbert to reconnoiter and see whether the people would be ready to rise, but Cuthbert found the Scots sunk in despair. All who had taken up arms had perished in the field or on the scaffold. The country swarmed with the English, and further resistance seemed hopeless. Cuthbert had arranged to light a beacon on a point at Turnberry visible from Lamlash Bay in Arran, where the king, with his two hundred men and eighty-three boats, awaited the sight of the smoke which should tell them that circumstances were favorable for their landing.

Cuthbert, finding that there was no chance of a

rising, did not light the bonfire; but as if fortune
was determined that Bruce should continue a struggle which was to end finally in the freedom of Scotland, some other person lit a fire on the very spot
where Cuthbert had arranged to show the signal.
On seeing the smoke the king and his party at once
got into their boats and rowed across to the mainland, a distance of seventeen miles. On reaching
land they were met by Cuthbert, who reported that
the fire was not of his kindling, and that the circumstances were altogether unfavorable. Bruce
consulted with his brother Edward, Douglas, Archie,
and his principal friends as to what course had
better be pursued. Edward declared at once that
he for one would not take to sea again; and this
decision settled the matter.

The king without delay led his followers against
the village outside the castle, where a considerable
portion of the garrison were housed. These were
assailed so suddenly that all save one were slain.
Those in the castle heard the sounds of the conflict,
but being unaware of the smallness of the assailant's force, did not venture to sally out to their
assistance.

Percy, with his followers, remained shut up in the
castle, while Bruce overran the neighboring country; but an English force under Sir Roger St. John,
far too powerful to be resisted, advanced to Turnberry, and Bruce and his followers were obliged to
seek refuge in the hills. Thomas and Alexander,
the king's brothers, with Sir Reginald Crawford,

had gone to the islands to beat up recruits, and returning in a vessel with a party who had joined
them, landed at Loch Ryan. They were attacked
at once by Macdowall, a chieftain of Galloway, and
routed. The king's brothers, with Sir Reginald
Crawford, were carried to Carlisle severely wounded
and delivered over to King Edward, who at once
sent them to the scaffold.

These wholesale and barbarous executions sad-
dened the Scots, and, as might be expected, soon
roused them to severe reprisals. Bruce himself,
however, although deeply stirred by the murder of
his three brothers and many dear friends, and by
the captivity and harsh treatment of his wife and
female relatives, never attempted to take vengeance
for them upon those who fell into his hands, and
during the whole of the war in no single instance
did he put a prisoner to death. He carried magnanimity, indeed, almost to the extent of impolicy ;
for had the nobles of England found that those of
their number who fell into Bruce's hands suffered
the penalty of death, which Edward inflicted upon
the Scotch prisoners, they would probably have remonstrated with the king and insisted upon his
conducting the war in a less barbarous and ferocious
fashion.

Sir James Douglas was so stirred by the murder
of the three Bruces and so many of his friends and
companions, that he resolved henceforth to wage an
exterminating war against the English, and by the
recapture of his own stronghold, known as Castle

Douglas, began the series of desperate deeds which won for him the name of the Black Douglas, and rendered his name for generations a terror among the English on the border. The castle had been conferred by Edward on Sir Robert de Clifford, and was occupied by an English garrison. Douglas revealed his intention only to Archie Forbes, who at once agreed to accompany him. He asked leave from the king to quit their hiding-place for a time, accompanied by Archie, in order to revisit Douglas Hall, and see how it fared with his tenants and friends. The king acquiesced with difficulty, as he thought the expedition a dangerous one, and feared that the youth and impetuosity of Douglas might lead him into danger ; before consenting he strongly urged on Archie to keep a strict watch over the doings of the young noble.

Accompanied by but one retainer, the friends set out for Douglasdale. When they arrived there Douglas went to the cottage of an old and faithful servant named Thomas Dickson, by whom he was joyfully received. Dickson went out among the retainers and revealed to such as could be most surely depended upon the secret of their lord's presence, and one by one took them in to see him. The friends had already determined upon their course, and the retainers all promised to take part in the scheme. They were not numerous enough to assault the castle openly, but they chose the following Sunday for the assault. This was Palm Sunday and a festival, and most of the garrison would come to the

Church of St. Bride, in the village of the same name, a short distance from the castle.

Dickson with some of his friends went at the appointed time, with arms concealed under their clothes, to the church; and ofter the service had commenced Douglas and some of his followers gathered outside. Unfortunately for the plan, some of those outside set up the shout, "A Douglas!" prematurely before the whole party had arrived and were ready to rush into the church. Dickson with his friends at once drew out their arms and attacked the English; but being greatly outnumbered and for a time unsupported, most of them, including their leader, were slain. Sir James and his followers then fought their way in, and after a desperate fight all the garrison save ten were killed.

The party then proceeded to the castle, which they captured without resistance. Douglas and his companions partook of the dinner which had been prepared for the garrison; then as much money, weapons, armor, and clothing as they could carry away was taken from the castle. The whole of the vast stores of provisions were carried into the cellar, the heads struck out of the ale and wine casks, the prisoners were slain and their bodies thrown down into the mass, and the castle was then set on fire. Archie Forbes in vain begged Douglas to spare the lives of the prisoners, but the latter would not listen to him. "No, Sir Archie," he exclaimed; "the King of England held my good father a prisoner in chains until he died; he has

The Black Douglas' revenge.—Page 290.

—In Freedom's Cause.

struck off the heads of every one of our friends who have fallen into his hands; he has wasted Scotland from end to end with fire and sword, and has slain our people in tens of thousands. So long as this war continues, so long will I slay every prisoner who falls into my hands, as King Edward would slay me did I fall into his; and I will not desist unless this cruel king agrees to show quarter to such of us as he may capture. I see not why all the massacring and bloodshed should be upon one side."

Archie did not urge him further, for he too was half beside himself with indignation and grief at the murder of the king's brothers and friends, and at the cruel captivity which, by a violation of the laws of sanctuary, had fallen upon the ladies with whom he had spent so many happy hours in the mountains and forests of Athole.

Douglas and Archie now rejoined the king. For months Bruce led the life of a hunted fugitive. His little following dwindled away until but sixty men remained in arms. Of these a portion were with the king's brother in Galloway, and with but a handful of men Bruce was lying among the fastnesses of Carrick when Sir Ingram de Umfraville, with a large number of troops sent by the Earl of Pembroke from Edinburgh, approached. Wholly unable to resist so large a force, Bruce's little party scattered, and the king himself, attended only by a page, lay hidden in the cottage of a peasant. The English in vain searched for him, until a traitorous

Scot went to Umfraville and offered, for a reward of a grant of land to the value of forty pounds annually, to slay Bruce.

The offer was accepted, and the traitor with his two sons made their way to Bruce's place of concealment. As they approached, Bruce snatched his bow from his page and shot the traitor through the eye. One son attacked him with an axe, but was slain with a blow from the king's sword. The remaining assailant rushed at him with a spear; but the king with one blow cut off the spear-head, and before the assailant had time to draw his sword, stretched him dead at his feet.

After this the king with his adherents eluded the search of the English and made their way into Galloway. The people here who were devoted to the English cause determined to hunt him down, and two hundred men, accompanied by some bloodhounds, set off toward the king's retreat; but Bruce's scouts were on the watch and brought him news of their coming. The king with his party retired until they reached a morass, through which flowed a running stream, while beyond, a narrow passage led through a deep quagmire.

Beyond this point the hunted party lay down to rest, while the king with two followers returned to the river to keep watch. After listening for some time they heard the baying of the hounds coming nearer and nearer, and then, by the light of a bright moon, saw their enemies approaching.

The king sent his two followers to rouse the band.

The enemy, seeing Bruce alone, pressed forward with all haste; and the king, knowing that if he retired his followers would be attacked unprepared, determined alone to defend the narrow path. He retired from the river bank to the spot where the path was narrowest and the morass most impassable, and then drew his sword. His pursuers, crossing the river, rode forward against him; Bruce charged the first, and with his lance slew him; then with a blow with his mace he stretched his horse beside him, blocking the narrow passage. One by one his foes advanced, and five fell beneath his blows before his companions ran up from behind. The Galloway men then took to flight, but nine more were slain before they could cross the ford.

The admiration and confidence of Bruce's followers were greatly aroused by this new proof of his courage and prowess. Sir James Douglas, his brother Edward, and others soon afterward returned from the expeditions on which they had been sent, and the king had now four hundred men assembled. This force, however, was powerless to resist an army of English and Lowland Scots who marched against him, led by Pembroke in person. This force was accompanied by John, son of Alexander Mac-Dougall of Lorne, with eight hundred of his mountaineers. While the heavy armed troops occupied all the lowlands, Lorne and his followers made a circuit in the mountains so as to inclose the royal fugitive between them.

Bruce, seeing that resistance was impossible,

caused his party to separate into three divisions, and Douglas, Edward Bruce, and Sir Archibald Forbes were charged to lead their bands, if possible, through the enemy without fighting. The king tried to escape by a different route with a handful of men. John of Lorne had obtained from Turn-berry a favorite bloodhound belonging to Bruce, and the hound being put upon the trace persistently followed the king's party. Seeing this, Bruce ordered them all to disperse, and, accompanied only by his foster-brother, attempted to escape by speed.

As they sped along the mountain side they were seen by Lorne, who directed his henchman, with four of his bravest and swiftest men, to follow him. After a long chase the MacDougalls came up with Bruce and his foster-brother, who drew their swords and stood on the defense. The henchman, with two of his followers, attacked Bruce, while the other two fell on his foster-brother. The combat was a desperate one, but one by one the king cut down his three assailants, and then turned to the assistance of his foster-brother, who was hardly pressed. The king's sword soon rid him of one of his assailants, and he slew the other. Having thus disembarrassed themselves of the whole of their immediate assailants, Bruce and his companion con-tined their flight. The main body of their hunters, with the hound, were but a short distance away, but in a wood the fugitives came upon a stream, and, marching for some distance down this, again landed, and continued their flight.

The hound lost their scent at the spot where they had entered the water, and being unable to recover it, Lorne and his followers abandoned the chase. Among the king's pursuers on this occasion was his nephew Randolph, who had been captured at the battle of Methven, and having again taken the oath of allegiance to Edward had been restored to that monarch's favor, and was now fighting among the English ranks.

The search was actively kept up after Bruce, and a party of three men-at-arms came upon him and his foster-brother. Being afraid to attack the king, whom they recognized, openly, they pretended they had come to join him.

The king suspected treachery; and when the five lay down for the night in a cottage which they came upon he and his companion agreed to watch alternately. Overcome by fatigue, however, both fell asleep, and when they were suddenly attacked by the three strangers, the foster-brother was killed before he could offer any resistance. The king himself, although wounded, managed to struggle to his feet, and then proved more than a match for his three treacherous assailants, all of whom, after a desperate struggle, he slew.

The next morning he continued his way, and by nightfall succeeded in joining the three bands, who had safely reached the rendezvous he had appointed.

A few hours after this exploit of Bruce, Archie with two or three of his followers joined him.

"This is indeed a serious matter of the hound," Archie said when Bruce told him how nearly he had fallen a victim to the affection of his favorite. "Methinks, sire, so long as he remains in the English hands your life will never be safe, for the dog will always lead the searchers to your hiding-places; if one could get near enough to shoot him, the danger would be at an end."

"I would not have him shot, Archie, for a large sum. I have had him since he was a little pup; he has for years slept across my door, and would give his life for mine. 'Tis but his affection now that brings danger upon me."

"I should be sorry to see the dog killed myself," Archie said, "for he is a fine fellow, and he quite admitted me to his friendship during the time we were together. Still, sire, if it were a question between their lives and yours, I would not hesitate to kill any number of dogs. The whole future of Scotland is wrapped up in you; and as there is not one of your followers but would gladly give his life for yours, it were no great thing that a hound should do the same."

"I cannot withstand you in argument, Archie," the king said, smiling; "yet I would fain that my favorite should, if possible, be spared. But I grant you should there be no other way, and the hound should continue to follow me, he must be put to death. But it would grieve me sorely. I have lost so many and so dear friends in the last year, that I can ill spare one of the few that are left me."

Archie was himself fond of dogs, and knowing how attached Bruce was to his faithful hound he could quite understand how reluctant he was that harm should come to him. Still, he felt it was necessary that the dog should, at all hazards, be either killed or taken from the English, for if he remained in their hands he was almost certain sooner or later to lead to Bruce's capture. He determined then to endeavor to avert the danger by abstracting the dog from the hands of the English, or, failing that, by killing him. To do this it would be absolutely necessary to enter the English camp. There was no possibility of carrying out his purpose without running this risk, for when in pursuit of the king the hound would be held by a leash, and there would be many men-at-arms close by, so that the difficulty of shooting him would be extremely great, and Archie could see no plan save that of boldly entering the camp.

He said nothing of his project to Bruce, who would probably have refused to allow him to undertake it; but the next morning when he parted from him—for it was considered advisable that the fugitives should be divided into the smallest groups, and that only one or two of his retainers should remain with Bruce—he started with his own followers in the direction of Pembroke's camp. He presently changed clothes with one of these, and they then collected a quantity of firewood and made it into a great fagot. Archie gave them orders where they should await him, and lifting the fagot on his

shoulders boldly entered the camp. He passed
with it near the pavilion of Pembroke. The earl
was standing with some knights at the entrance.

"Come hither, Scot," he said as Archie passed.

Archie laid his bundle on the ground, and doffing
his bonnet strode with an awkward and abashed air
toward the earl.

" I suppose you are one of Bruce's men ?" the earl
said.

" My father," Archie replied, "as well as all who
dwell in these dales, were his vassals ; but seeing
that, as they say, his lands have been forfeit and
given to others, I know not whose man I am at
present."

" Dost know Bruce by figure ?"

"Surely," Archie said simply, " seeing that I was
employed in the stables at Turnberry, and used to
wash that big hound of his, who was treated as
a Christian rather than a dog."

"Oh, you used to tend the hound !" Pembroke
said.   "Then perhaps you could manage him now.
He is here in camp, and the brute is so savage
and fierce he has already well-nigh killed two
or three men ; and I would have had him shot but
that he may be useful to us.   If he knows you he
may be quieter with you than others."

"Doubtless he would know me," Archie said ;
"but seeing that I have the croft to look after, as
my father is old and infirm, I trust that you will
excuse me the service of looking after the hound."

" Answer me not," Pembroke said angrily. " You

may think yourself lucky, seeing that you are one of Bruce's retainers, that I do not have you hung from a tree. Take the fellow to the hound," he said to one of his retainers, "and see if the brute recognizes him; if so put him in charge of him for the future. And see you, Scot, that you attempt no tricks, for if you try to escape I will hang you without shrift."

Archie followed the earl's retainer to where, behind his pavilion, the great dog was chained up. He leaped to his feet with a savage growl on hearing footsteps approaching. His hair bristled and he tugged at his chain.

"What a savage beast it is!" the man said; "I would sooner face a whole company of you Scots than get within reach of his jaws. Dickon," he went on, as another soldier, on hearing the growl, issued from one of the smaller tents which stood in rear of the pavilion, "the earl has sent this Scot to relieve you of your charge of the dog; he is to have the care of him in future."

"That is the best turn the earl has done me for a long time," the man replied. "Never did I have a job I fancied less than the tending of that evil-tempered brute."

"He did not use to be evil-tempered," Archie said; "but was a quiet beast when I had to do with him before. I suppose the strangeness of the place and so many strange faces have driven him half wild. Besides, he is not used to being chained up. Hector, old fellow," he said, approaching the dog quietly, "don't you know me?"

The great hound recognized the voice and his aspect changed at once. The bristling hair lay flat on his back; the threatening jaws closed. He gave a short, deep bark of pleasure, and then began leaping and tugging at his chain to reach his acquaintance. Archie came close to him now. Hector reared on his hind legs, and placed his great paws on his shoulders, and licked his face with whines of joy.

"He knows you, sure enough," the man said; "and maybe we shall get on better now. At any rate there may be some chance of sleep, for the brute's howls every night since he has been brought here have kept the whole camp awake."

"No wonder!" Archie said, "when he has been accustomed to be petted and cared for; he resents being chained up."

"Would you unchain him?" the man asked.

"That would I," Archie replied; "and I doubt not that he will stay with me."

"It may be so," the man replied; "but you had best not unchain him without leave from the earl, for were he to take it into his head to run away I would not give a groat for your life. But I will go and acquaint the earl that the dog knows you, and ask his orders as to his being unchained."

In two or three minutes he returned.

"The earl says that on no account is he to be let free. He has told me to have a small tent pitched here for you. The hound is to be chained to the post, and to share the tent with you. You may, if you will, walk about the camp with him, but always keeping him in a chain; but if you do so it will be at your peril, for if he gets away your life will answer for it."

In a short time two or three soldiers brought a small tent and erected it close by where the dog was chained up. Archie unloosed the chain from the post round which it was fastened, and led Hector to the tent, the dog keeping close by his side and wagging his tail gravely, as if to show his appreciation of the change, to the satisfaction of the men to whom hitherto he had been a terror.

Some heather was brought for a bed, and a supply of food, both for the dog and his keeper, and the men then left the two friends alone. Hector was sitting up on his haunches gazing affectionately at Archie, his tail beating the ground with slow and regular strokes.

"I know what you want to ask, old fellow," Archie said to him; "why I don't lead you at once to your master? Don't you be impatient, old fellow, and you shall see him ere long;" and he patted the hound's head.

Hector, with a great sigh expressive of content and satisfaction, lay down on the ground by the side of the couch of heather on which Archie threw himself—his nose between his forepaws, clearly expressing that he considered his troubles were over, and could now afford to wait until in due time he should be taken to his master. That night the camp slept quietly, for Hector was silent.

For the next two days Archie did not go more than a few yards from his tent, for he feared that he might meet some one who would recognize him.

CHAPTER XVIII.

THE HOUND RESTORED.

ON THE third day after his arrival at the camp Archie received orders to prepare to start with the hound, with the earl and a large party of men-at-arms, in search of Bruce. A traitor had just come in and told them where Bruce had slept the night before. Reluctantly Archie unfastened the chain from the pole, and holding the end in his hand went round with Hector to the front of the pavilion. He was resolved that if under the dog's guidance the party came close up with Bruce, he would kill the dog and then try to escape by fleetness of foot, though of this, as there were so many mounted men in the party, he had but slight hope. Led by the peasant they proceeded to the hut, which was five miles away in the hills. On reaching it Hector at once became greatly excited. He sniffed here and there, eagerly hunted up and down the cottage, then made a circuit round it, and at last, with a loud deep bay he started off with his nose to the ground, pulling so hard at the chain that Archie had difficulty in keeping up with him.

Pembroke and his knights rode a little behind, followed by their men-at-arms.

"I pray you, sir earl," Archie said, "keep not too close to my traces, for the sound of the horses' hoofs, and the jingling of the equipments make him all the more impatient to get forward, and even now it taxes all my strength to hold him in."

The earl reined back his horse and followed at a distance of some fifty yards. He had no suspicion whatever of any hidden design on Archie's part. The fact that the hound had recognized him had appeared to him a sure proof of the truth of his tale, and Archie had put on an air of such stupid simplicity that the earl deemed him to have but imperfect possession of his wits. Moreover, in any case he could overtake him in case he attempted flight.

Archie proceeded at a trot behind the hound, who was with difficulty restrained at that pace, straining eagerly on the chain and occasionally sending out his deep bay. Archie anxiously regarded the country through which he was passing. He was waiting for an opportunity, and was determined, whenever they passed near a steep hillside unscalable by horsemen, he would stab Hector to the heart and take to flight. Presently he saw a man, whose attire showed him to be a Highlander, approaching at a run; he passed close by Archie, and as he did so stopped suddenly, exclaiming, "Archibald Forbes!" and drawing his broadsword sprang at him. Archie, who was unarmed save by a long

knife, leaped back. In the man he recognized the
leader of the MacDougall's party, who had captured
him near Dunstaffnage. The conflict would have
terminated in an instant had not Hector intervened.
Turning round with a deep growl the great hound
sprang full at the throat of the Highlander as with
uplifted sword he rushed at Archie. The impetus
of the spring threw the MacDougall on his back,
with the fangs of the hound fixed in his throat.

Archie's first impulse was to pull the dog off, the
second thought showed him that, were the man to
survive he would at once denounce him. Accordingly, though he appeared to tug hard at Hector's
chain, he in reality allowed him to have his way.
Pembroke and his knights instantly galloped up.
As they arrived Hector loosed his hold, and with
his hair bristly with rage prepared to attack those
whom he regarded as fresh enemies.

"Hold in that hound," Pembroke shouted, "or he
will do more damage. What means all this?" For
a minute Archie did not answer, being engaged in
pacifying Hector, who, on seeing that no harm was
intended, strove to return to his first foe.

"It means," Archie said, when Hector was at last
pacified, "that that Highlander came the other day
to our cottage and wanted to carry off a cow without making payment for it. I withstood him, he
drew his sword, but as I had a stout cudgel in my
hand I hit him on the wrist ere he could use it, and
well-nigh broke his arm. So he made off, cursing
and swearing, and vowing that the next time he
met me he would have my life."

" And that he would have done," Pembroke said,
" had it not been for Bruce's dog, who has turned
matters the other way. He is dead assuredly. It
is John of Lorne's henchman, who was doubtless on
his way with a message from his lord to me. Could
not the fool have postponed his grudge till he had
delivered it? I tell you, Scot, you had best keep
out of the MacDougalls' way, for assuredly they
will revenge the death of their clansman upon you
if they have the chance, though I can testify that
the affair was none of your seeking. Now let us
continue our way."

" I doubt me, sir earl, whether our journey ends
not here," Archie said, " seeing that these hounds,
when they taste blood, seem for a time to lose their
fineness of scent; but we shall see."

Archie's opinion turned out correct. Do what
they would they could not induce Hector again to
take up his master's trail, the hound again and
again returning to the spot where the dead Highlander still lay. Pembroke had the body carried
off; but the hound tugged at his chain in the direction in which it had gone, and seemed to have lost
all remembrance of the track upon which he was
going. At last Pembroke was obliged to acknowledge that is was useless to pursue longer, and, full
of disappointment at their failure, the party
returned to camp, Pembroke saying: " Our chase
is but postponed. We are sure to get tidings
of Bruce's hiding-place in a day or two, and next
time we will have the hound muzzled, lest any hot-

headed Highlander should again interfere to mar the sport."

It was some days before further tidings were obtained of Bruce. Archie did not leave his tent during this time, giving as a reason that he was afraid if he went out he should meet some of Lorne's men, who might take up the quarrel of the man who had been killed. At length, however, another traitor came in, and Pembroke and his party set out as before, Hector being this time muzzled by a strap round his jaw, which would not interfere with his scent, but would prevent him from widely opening his jaws.

The scent of Bruce was again taken up at a lonely hut in the hills. The country was far more broken and rough than that through which they had followed Bruce's trail on the preceding occasion. Again Archie determined, but most reluctantly, that he would slay the noble dog; but he determined to postpone the deed to the latest moment. Several places were passed where he might have succeeded in effecting his escape after stabbing the hound, but each time his determination failed him. It would have been of no use to release the dog and make himself up the hillside, for a bloodhound's pace when on the track is not rapid, and the horsemen could have kept up with Hector, who would of course have continued his way upon the trail of the king. Presently two men were seen in the distance; they had evidently been alarmed by the bay of the hound, and were going at full speed. A shout of triumph broke from the pursuers, and some of the more eager would have set spurs to their horses and passed the hound.

"Rein back, rein back," Pembroke said; "the country is wild and hilly here, and Bruce may hide himself long before you can overtake him. Keep steadily in his track till he gains flatter country, where we can keep him in sight, then we shall have no more occasion for the hound and can gallop on at full speed."

Archie observed, with satisfaction, that Bruce was making up an extremely steep hillside, deeming probably that horsemen would be unable to follow him here, and that he would be able to distance pursuers on foot. Ten minutes later his pursuers had reached the foot of the hill. Pembroke at once ordered four knights and ten men-at-arms to dismount.

"Do you," he said, "with the dog, follow hard upon the traces of Bruce. When you reach the top signal to us the direction in which he has gone. Follow ever on his track without stopping ; he must at last take to the low country again. Some of my men shall remain here, others a mile further on, and so on round the whole foot of the hills. Do you, when you see that, thinking he has distanced you, which he may well do being more lightly armed and flying for his life, he makes for the low country again, send men in different directions to give me warning. The baying of the dog will act as a signal to us."

Archie baffles his pursuers.—Page 309.

—In *Freedom's Cause.*

While the men had been dismounting and Pembroke was giving his orders Archie had proceeded up the hill with the hound. The path was exceedingly steep and difficult.

"Do not hurry, sirrah," Pembroke called; "hold in your hound till the others join you." But Archie paid no attention to the shout, but kept up the steep path at the top of his speed. Shouts and threats followed him, but he paused not till he reached the top of the ascent; then he unfastened Hector's collar, and the dog, relieved from the chain which had so long restrained him, bounded away with a deep bay in pursuit of his master, whose scent was now strong before him. As Archie looked back, the four knights and their followers, in single file, were, as yet, scarce halfway up the ascent. Lying round were numbers of loose boulders, and Archie at once began to roll these down the hillside. They went but slowly at first, but as they reached the steeper portion they gathered speed, and taking great bounds crashed down the hillside. As these formidable missiles burst down from above the knights paused.

"On!" Pembroke shouted from below; "the Scot is a traitor, and he and the hound will escape if you seize him not." Again the party hurried up the hill. Three of them were struck down by the rocks, and the speed of all was impeded by the pauses made to avoid the great boulders which bounded down toward them. When they were within a few yards of the top Archie turned and bounded off at full speed.　He had no fear of being himself overtaken.　Lightly clad and unarmed, the knights and men-at-arms, who were all in full armor, and who were already breathed with the exertions they had made, would have no chance of overtaking him; indeed he could safely have fled at once when he loosed Hector, but he had stopped to delay the ascent of his pursuers solely to give the hound as long a start as possible.　He himself could have kept up with the hound; the men-at-arms could assuredly not do so, but they might for a long time keep him in sight, and his baying would afterward indicate the line the king was taking, and Bruce might yet be cut off by the mounted men.　The delay which his bombardment had caused had given a long start to the hound, for it was more than five minutes from the time when it had been loosed before the pursuers gained the crest of the hill.　Archie, in his flight, took a different line to that which the dog had followed.　Hector was already out of sight, and although his deep baying might for a time afford an index to his direction this would soon cease to act as a guide, as the animal would rapidly increase his distance from his pursuers, and would, when he had overtaken the king, cease to emit his warning note.　The pursuers, after a moment's pause for consultation on the crest of the hill, followed the line taken by the hound.

The men-at-arms paused to throw aside their defensive armor, breast, back, and leg pieces, and the

knights relieved themselves of some of their iron
gear; but the delay, short as it was, caused by the
unbuckling of straps and unlacing of helms, increased the distance which already existed between
them and the hound, whose deep notes, occasionally
raised, grew fainter and fainter. In a few minutes
it ceased altogether, and Archie judged that the
hound had overtaken his master, who, on seeing the
animal approaching alone, would naturally have
checked his flight. Archie himself was now far
away from the men-at-arms, and after proceeding
until beyond all reach of pursuit, slackened his
pace, and breaking into a walk continued his course
some miles across the hills until he reached a lonely
cottage where he was kindly received and remained
until next day.

The following morning he set out and journeyed
to the spot where, on leaving his retainers more
than a week before, he had ordered them to await
his coming. It was another week before he obtained such news as enabled him again to join the
king, who was staying at a woodcutter's hut in
Selkirk Forest. Hector came out with a deep bark
of welcome.

"Well, Sir Archie," the king said, following his
dog to the door, "and how has it fared with you
since we last parted a fortnight since? I have been
hotly chased, and thought I should have been
taken; but, thanks to the carelessness of the fellow
who led my hound, Hector somehow slipped his
collar and joined me, and I was able to shake off

my pursuers, so that danger is over, and without
sacrificing the life of my good dog."

Archie smiled. "Perchance, sire, it was not from
any clumsiness that the hound got free, but that he
was loosed by some friendly hand."

"It may be so," the king replied; "but they
would scarcely have intrusted him to a hand friendly
to me. Nor would his leader, even if so disposed,
have ventured to slip the hound, seeing that the
horsemen must have been close by at the time, and
that such a deed would cost him his life. It was
only because Hector got away, when the horsemen
were unable to follow him, that he escaped, seeing
that, good dog as he is, speed is not his strong
point, and that horsemen could easily gallop alongside of him even were he free. What are you smiling at, Sir Archie? The hound and you seem on
wondrous friendly terms;" for Hector was now
standing up with his great paws on Archie's
shoulder.

"So we should be, sire, seeing that for eight days
we have shared bed and board."

"Ah! is it so?" Bruce exclaimed. "Was it you,
then, that loosed the hound?"

"It was, sire," Archie replied; "and this is the
history of it; and you will see that if I have done
you and Hector a service in bringing you together
again the hound has repaid it by saving my life."

Entering the hut, Archie sat down and related
all that had happened to the king.

"You have done me great service, Sir Archie,"

Bruce said when he concluded his tale, "for assuredly the hound would have wrought my ruin had he remained in the hands of the English. This is another of the long list of services you have rendered me. Some day, when I come to my own, you will find that I am not ungrateful."

The feats which have been related of Bruce, and other personal adventures in which he distinguished himself, won the hearts of great numbers of the Scotch people. They recognized now that they had in him a champion as doughty and as valiant as Wallace himself. The exploits of the king filled their imaginations, and the way in which he continued the struggle after the capture of the ladies of his family and the cruel execution of his brothers and so many of his adherents, convinced them that he would never desist until he was dead or a conqueror. Once persuaded of this, larger numbers gathered round his banner, and his fortunes henceforth began steadily to rise.

Lord Clifford had rebuilt Douglas Castle, making it larger and stronger than before, and had committed it to the charge of Captain Thirlwall, with a strong garrison. Douglas took a number of his retainers, who had now joined him in the field, and some of these, dressing themselves as drovers and concealing their arms, drove a herd of cattle within sight of the castle toward an ambuscade in which Douglas and the others were lying in ambush. The garrison, seeing what they believed a valuable prize within their grasp, sallied out to seize the cattle.

When they reached the ambuscade the Scots sprang out upon them, and Thirlwall and the greater portion of his men were slain. Douglas then took and destroyed the castle and marched away. Clifford again rebuilt it more strongly than before, and placed it in charge of Sir John Walton. It might have been thought that after the disasters which had befallen the garrison they would not have suffered themselves to be again entrapped. Douglas, however, ordered a number of his men to ride past within sight of the castle with sacks upon their horses, apparently filled with grain, but in reality with grass, as if they were countrymen on their way to the neighboring market town, while once more he and his followers placed themselves in ambush.

Headed by their captain, the garrison poured out from the castle, and followed the apparent country-men until they had passed the ambush where Douglas was lying. Then the drovers threw off their disguises and attacked them, while Douglas fell upon their rear, and Walton and his companions were all slain. The castle was then attacked, and the remainder of the garrison being cowed by the fate which had befallen their leader and comrades, made but a poor defense. The castle was taken, and was again destroyed by its lord, the walls being, as far as possible, overthrown.

Shortly after the daring adventures of Bruce had begun to rouse the spirit of the country Archie Forbes found himself at the head of a larger following than before. Foreseeing that the war must be a long one he had called upon his tenants and retainers to furnish him only with a force one-third of that of their total strength. Thus he was able to maintain sixty men always in the field—all the older men on the estate being exempted from service unless summoned to defend the castle.

One day when he was in the forest of Selkirk with the king a body of fifty men were seen approaching. Their leader inquired for Sir Archibald Forbes, and presently approached him as he was talking to the king.

"Sir Archibald Forbes," he said, "I am bidden by my mistress, the lady Mary Kerr, to bring these a portion of the retainers of her estates in Ayrshire, and to place them in your hands to lead and govern."

"In my hands!" Archie exclaimed in astonishment. "The Kerrs are all on the English side, and I am their greatest enemy. It were strange, indeed, were one of them to choose me to lead their retainers in the cause of Scotland."

"Our young lord Sir Allan was slain at Methven," the man said, "and the lady Mary is now our lady and mistress. She sent to us months ago to say that she willed not that any of her retainers should any longer take part in the struggle, and all who were in the field were summoned home. Then we heard that no hindrance would be offered by her should any wish to join the Bruce; and now she has sent by a messenger a letter under her hand order-

ing that a troop of fifty men shall be raised to join
the king, and that it shall fight under the leading
and order of Sir Archibald Forbes."

"I had not heard that Sir Allan had fallen,"
Archie said to the king as they walked apart from
the place where the man was standing; "and in
truth I had forgotten that he even had a sister. She
must have been a child when I was a boy at Glen
Cairn, and could have been but seldom at the castle
—which, indeed, was no fit abode for so young a
girl, seeing that Sir John's wife had died some
years before I left Glen Cairn. Perhaps she was
with her mother's relations. I have heard that Sir
John Kerr married a relation of the Comyns of
Badenoch. 'Tis strange if, being of such bad blood
on both sides, she should have grown up a true
Scotchwoman—still more strange she should send
her vassals to fight under the banner of one whom
she must regard as the unlawful holder of her
father's lands of Aberfilly."

"Think you, Sir Archie," the king said, "that this
is a stratagem, and that these men have really come
with a design to seize upon you and slay you, or to
turn traitors in the first battle?"

Archie was silent. "Treachery has been so much
at work," he said after a pause, "that it were rash
to say that this may not be a traitorous device; but
it were hard to think that a girl—even a Kerr—
would lend herself to it."

"There are bad women as well as bad men," the
king said; "and if a woman thinks she has

grievances she will often stick at nothing to obtain revenge."

"It is a well-appointed troop," Archie said, looking at the men, who were drawn up in order, "and not to be despised. Their leader looks an honest fellow; and if the lady means honestly it were churlish indeed to refuse her aid when she ventures to break with her family and to declare for Scotland. No; methinks that, with your permission, I will run the risk, such as it may be, and will join this band with my own. I will keep a sharp watch over them at the first fight, and will see that they are so placed that, should they mean treachery, they shall have but small opportunity of doing harm."

CHAPTER XIX.

THE CONVENT OF ST. KENNETH.

BRUCE, as the result of his successes, was now able to leave his fastnesses and establish himself in the districts of Carrick, Kyle, and Cunningham. Pembroke had established himself at Bothwell Castle, and sent a challenge to Bruce to meet him with his force at Loudon Hill. Although his previous experience of such challenges was unfortunate, Bruce accepted the offer. He had learned much since the battle of Methven, and was not likely again to be caught asleep; on the 9th of May he assembled his forces at Loudon Hill.

It was but a small following. Douglas had brought one hundred men from Douglasdale, and Archie Forbes had as many under his banner. Bruce's own vassals had gathered two hundred strong, and as many more of the country people had joined; but in all, the Scotch force did not exceed six hundred men, almost entirely on foot and armed with spears. Bruce at once reconnoitered the ground to discover a spot where his little force might best withstand the shock of Pembroke's chivalry. He found that at one place near the hill the road crossed a level meadow with deep morasses on either side. He strengthened the position with trenches, and calmly awaited the approach of his enemy.

Upon the following day Pembroke's army was seen approaching, numbering three thousand knights and mounted men-at-arms, all in complete armor. They were formed in two divisons. The battle was almost a repetition of that which had been fought by Wallace near the same spot. The English chivalry leveled their spears and charged with proud confidence of their ability to sweep away the rabble of spearmen in front of them. Their flanks became entangled in the morasses; their center tried in vain to break through the hedge of Scottish spears, and when they were in confusion, the king, his brother Edward, Douglas Archie Forbes, and some twenty other mounte men dashed through a gap in the spearmen and fel. upon them. The second division, seeing the first broken and in confusion, turned and took to flight at once, and Pembroke and his attendants rode, without drawing rein, to Bothwell Castle.

A few days later Bruce encountered and defeated Ralph de Monthermer, Earl of Gloucester, and compelled him to shut himself up in the Castle of Ayr.

Archie Forbes was not present at the second battle, for upon the morning after the fight at Loudon Hill he was aroused by his servant entering his tent.

"A messenger has just brought this," he said, handing him a small packet. "He bids me tell you that the sender is a prisoner in the convent of St. Kenneth, on Loch Leven, and prays your aid."

Archie opened the packet and found within it the ring he had given to Marjory at Dunstaffnage. Without a moment's delay he hurried to the king and begged permission to leave him for a short time on urgent business, taking with him twenty of his retainers.

"What is your urgent business, Sir Archie?" the king asked. "A lady is in the case, I warrant me. Whenever a young knight has urgent business, be sure that a lady is in question. Now mind, Sir Archie, I have, as I have told you, set my heart upon marrying you to Mistress Mary Kerr, and so at once putting an end to a long feud and doubling your possessions. Her retainers fought well yesterday, and the least I can do to reward so splendid a damsel is to bestow upon her the hand of my bravest knight."

"I fear, sire," Archie said, laughing, "that she must be content with another. There are plenty who will deem themselves well paid for their services in your cause by the gift of the hand of so rich an heiress. But I must fain be excused; for as I told you, sire, when we were together in Rathlin Island, my heart was otherwise bestowed."

"What! to the niece of that malignant enemy of mine, Alexander of Lorne?" the king said, laughing. "Her friends would rather see you on the gibbet than at the altar."

"I care nought for her friends," Archie said, "if I can get herself. My own lands are wide enough, and I need no dowry with my wife."

"I see you are hopeless," the king replied. "Well go, Archie; but whatever be your errand, beware of the Lornes. Remember I have scarce begun to win Scotland yet, and cannot spare you."

A quarter of an hour later Archie, with twenty picked men, took his way northward. Avoiding all towns and frequented roads, Archie marched rapidly north to the point of Renfrew and crossed the Frith of Clyde by boat; then he kept north round the head of Loch Fyne, and avoiding Dalmally skirted the head of Loch Etive and the slopes of Ben Nevis, and so came down on Loch Leven.

The convent stood at the extremity of a promontory jutting into the lake. The neck was very narrow, and across it were strong walls, with a gate and flanking towers. Between this wall and the convent was the garden where the inmates walked and enjoyed the air free from the sight of men, save, indeed, of fishers who might be passing in their boats.

Outside the wall, on the shore of the lake, stood a large village; and here a strong body of the retainers of the convent were always on guard, for at St. Kenneth were many of the daughters of Scotch nobles, sent there either to be out of the way during the troubles or to be educated by the nuns. Although the terrors of sacrilege and the ban of the church might well deter any from laying hands upon the convent, yet even in those days of superstition some were found so fierce and irreverent as to dare even the anger of the church to carry out their wishes ; and the possession of some of these heiresses might well enable them to make good terms for themselves both with the church and the relations of their captives. Therefore a number of the retainers were always under arms, a guard was placed on the gate, and lookouts on the flanking towers— their duty being not only to watch the land side, but to shout orders to keep at a distance to any fisherman who might approach too closely to the promontory.

Archie left his party in the forest under the command of William Orr. He dressed himself as a mountaineer, and, accompanied by Cluny Campbell, and carrying a buck which they had shot in the forest, went boldly down into the village. He soon got into conversation with an old fisherman, and offered to exchange the deer for dried fish. The bargain was quickly struck, and then Archie said :

"I have never been out on the lake, and would fain have a view of the convent from the water. Will you take me and my brother out for a row ?"

The fisherman, who had made a good bargain, at once assented, and rowed Archie and Cluny far out into the lake.

As they passed along at some distance Archie saw that the shore was in several places smooth and shelving, and that there would be no difficulty in effecting a landing. He saw also that there were many clumps of trees and shrubs in the garden.

"And do the nuns and the ladies at the convent often walk there?" he asked the fisherman.

"Oh, yes," he answered; "of an evening as I come back from fishing I can see numbers of them walking there. When the vesper-bell rings they all go in. That is the chapel adjoining the convent on this side."

"It is a strong building," Archie said, as when past the end of the promontory they obtained a full view of it. "It is more like a castle than a convent."

"It had need be strong," the old man said; "for some of the richest heiresses in Scotland are shut up there. On the land side I believe there are no windows on the lower story, and the door is said to be of solid iron. The windows on that side are all strongly barred; and he would have hard work, indeed, who wanted by force or stratagem to steal one of the pretty birds out of that cage."

Archie had no idea of using force; and although he had been to some extent concerned in the breach of sanctuary at Dumfries, he would have shrunk from the idea of violating the sanctuary of St. Kenneth. But to his mind there was no breach whatever of that sanctuary in aiding one kept there against her will to make her escape. Having ascertained all that he wished to know, he bade the boatman return to shore.

"Keep a lookout for me," he said, "for I may return in a few days with another buck, and may bring a comrade or two with me who would like an afternoon's fishing on the lake. I suppose you could lend me your boat and nets ?"

"Assuredly," the fisherman replied. "You will not mind taking into consideration the hire of the boat in agreeing for the weight of fish to be given for the stag ?"

Archie nodded, secretly amused at the old man's covetousness, for he knew that the weight of fish he had given him for the stag which he had brought down was not one-fourth the value of the meat.

He then returned with Cluny to the band. Some time before daybreak he came down to the place again, and, entering the water quietly, at a distance from the promontory, swam noiselessly out, and landed at the garden, and there concealed himself in a clump of bushes.

Daylight came. An hour later some of the nuns of the second order, who belonged to poor families and acted as servants in the convent, came out into the garden, and busied themselves with the cultivation of the flowers, vegetables, and herbs. Not till the afternoon did any of the other inmates appear ; but at about four o'clock the great door of the convent opened, and a number of women and girls streamed out. The former were all in nuns' attire, as were a few of the latter, but their garb was somewhat different from that of the elder sisters ; these were the novices. The greater number, however, of the girls were dressed in ordinary attire, and were the pupils of the convent. While the nuns walked quietly up and down or sat on benches and read, the pupils scattered in groups, laughing and talking merrily together. Among these Archie looked eagerly for Marjory. He felt sure that her imprisonment could be detention only, and not rigorous seclusion. Presently he espied her. She was walking with two of the nuns and three or four of the elder residents at the convent, for many of these were past the age of pupildom, and were there simply as a safe place of refuge during troublous times. The conversation appeared to be an animated one. It was not for some time that the group passed within hearing of Archie's place of concealment. Then Archie heard the voice of one of the nuns raised in anger:

"It is monstrous what you say, and it is presumptuous and wicked for a young girl of eighteen to form opinions for herself. What should we come to if every young woman were to venture to think and judge for herself? Discord and disorder would be wrought in every family. All your relations and friends are opposed to this sacrilegious murderer, Robert Bruce. The church has solemnly banned him, and yet you venture to uphold his cause."

"But the Bishop of Glasgow," Marjory said, "and many other good prelates of our church side with him, and surely they must be good judges whether his sins are unpardonable."

"Do not argue with me," the sister said angrily. "I tell you this obstinacy will be permitted no longer. Had it not been that Alexander of Lorne begged that we would not be harsh with you, steps would long since have been taken to bring you to reason; but we can no longer permit this advocacy of rebellion, and the last unmaidenly step which you took of setting at defiance your friends and relatives, and even of sending messages hence, must be punished. The abbess bade me reason with you and try and turn your obstinate will. Your cousins of Badenoch here have appealed to you in vain. This can no longer be tolerated. The lady abbess bids me tell you that she gives you three days to renounce the rebel opinions you have so frowardly held, and to accept the husband whom your uncle and guardian has chosen for you, your cousin John of Lorne, his son. During that time none will speak to you. If at the end of three days you are still contumacious you will be confined to your cell on bread and water until better thoughts come to you."

While the conversation had been going on, the little group had halted near the bushes, and they now turned away, leaving Marjory standing by herself. The girl sat down on a bench close to where she had been standing, exclaiming to herself as she did so, "They may shut me up as a prisoner for life, but I will never consent to take sides against the cause of Scotland or to marry John of Lorne. Oh! who is there?" she exclaimed, starting suddenly to her feet as a man's voice behind her said:

"Quite right, Mistress Marjory, well and bravely resolved; but pray sit down again, and assume an attitude of indifference."

"Who is it that speaks?" the girl asked in a tremulous voice, resuming her seat.

"It is your true knight, lady, Archibald Forbes, who has come to rescue you from this captivity."

"But how can you rescue me?" the girl asked after a long pause. "Do you know the consequences if you are found here within the bounds of the convent?"

"I care nothing for the consequences," Archie said. "I have in the woods twenty stout followers. I propose to-morrow to be with three of them on the lake a-fishing. If you, when the bell rings for your return in the evening, will enter that little copse by the side of the lake, and will show yourself at the water's edge, we will row straight in and take you off long ere the guards can come hither to hinder us. The lake is narrow, and we can reach the other side before any boat can overtake us. There my followers will be awaiting us, and we can escort you to a place of safety. It is fortunate that you are ordered to be apart from the rest; none therefore will mark you as you linger behind when the bell rings for vespers."

Marjory was silent for some time.

"But, sir knight," she said, "whither am I to go? for of all my friends not one, save the good priest, but is leagued against me."

"I can take you either to the Bishop of Glasgow, who is a friend of the Bruce and whom I know well —he will, I am sure, take charge of you—or, if you will, lady, I can place you with my mother, who will receive you as a daughter."

"But what," the girl said hesitatingly, "will people say at my running away from a convent with a young knight?"

"Let them say what they will," Archie said. "All good Scots, when they know that you have been in prison here solely from the love of your country, will applaud the deed; and should you prefer it, the king will, I know, place you in charge of the wife of one of the nobles who adheres to him, and will give you his protection and countenance. Think, lady, if you do not take this opportunity of gaining your freedom, it may never occur again, for if you are once shut up in your cell, as I heard threatened, nothing save an attack by force of arms, which would be sheer sacrilege, can rescue you from it. Surely," he urged, as the girl still remained silent, "you can trust yourself with me. Do I not owe my life to you? and I swear that so long as you remain in my charge I will treat you as my sister in all honor and respect."

For some minutes the girl made no answer. At length she said, standing up, and half turning toward the bushes:

"I will trust you, Sir Archie. I know you to be a brave and honorable knight, and I will trust you. I know 'tis a strange step to take, and the world will blame me; but what can I do? If I refuse your offer I shall be kept a prisoner here until I consent to marry John of Lorne, whom I hate, for he is as rough and cruel as his father, without the kindness of heart, which, save in his angry moments, the latter has ever had toward me. All my relations are against me, and struggle against my fate as I may, I must in the end bend to their will if I remain here. 'Tis a hard choice to make; but what can I do? Yes, I will trust to your honor; and may God and all the saints punish you if you are false to the trust! To-morrow evening, as the vespers are chiming, I will be at the water's edge, behind yonder clump of bushes."

Then, with head bent down and slow steps, Marjory returned to the convent, none addressing her as she passed through the groups of her companions, the order that she was to be shut out from the rest having been already issued. Archie remained in his place of concealment until the gardens were deserted and night had fallen. Then he left his hiding-place, and, entering the lake, swam quietly away, and landed far beyond the village. An hour's walk brought him to the encampment of his comrades.

At daybreak next morning the band, under the command of William Orr, started for their long march round the head of the lake to the position which they were to take up on the opposite side facing the convent, Archie choosing three of the number most accustomed to the handling of oars to remain with him. With these he set out on a hunt as soon as the main body had left, and by midday had succeeded in killing a stag. With this swung on a pole carried by his followers Archie proceeded to the village. He speedily found the fisherman with whom he had before bargained.

"I did not expect you back again so soon," the old man said.

"We killed a buck this morning," Archie said carelessly, "and my friends thought that the afternoon would be fine for fishing."

"You can try if you like," the fisherman said, "but I fear that you will have but little sport. The day is too bright and clear, and the fish will be sulking at the bottom of the lake."

"We will try," Archie said, "nevertheless. Even if the sport is bad it will be pleasant out on the lake, and if we catch nothing we will get you to give us some fresh fish instead of dry. The folks in the hills will be no wiser, and it will not do for us to return empty-handed."

The fisherman assented, and placed the oars and nets in the boat, and Archie and his companions entering rowed out into the middle of the lake, and then throwing over the nets busied themselves with fishing.

As the old man had predicted, their sport was but small, but this concerned them little. Thinking that they might be watched, they continued steadily all the afternoon casting and drawing in the nets, until the sun neared the horizon. Then they gathered the nets into the boat and rowed quietly toward the shore. Just as they were abreast the end of the promontory the bell of the chapel began to ring the vespers. A few more strokes and Archie could see the clump of bushes.

"Row quietly now," he said, still steering toward the village.

He was about a hundred yards distant from the shore of the convent garden. Just as he came abreast of the bushes the foliage was parted and Marjory appeared at the edge of the water. In an instant the boat's head was turned toward shore, and the three rowers bent to their oars.

A shout from the watchman on the turret showed that he had been watching the boat and that this sudden change of its course had excited his alarm. The shout was repeated again and again as the boat neared the shore, and just as the keel grated on the sand the outer gate was opened and some armed men were seen running into the garden, but they were still two hundred yards away. Marjory leaped lightly into the boat; the men pushed off, and before the retainers of the convent reached the spot the boat was speeding away over the lake. Archie gave up to Marjory his seat in the stern, and himself took an oar.

Loch Leven, though of considerable length, is narrow, and the boat was nearly a third of the way across it before two or three craft were seen putting out from the village in pursuit, and although these gained somewhat, the fugitives reached the other shore a long distance in advance. William Orr and his men were at the landing-place, and soon the whole party were hurrying through the wood. They had no fear of instant pursuit, for even in the fast gathering gloom those in the boats would have perceived the accession of force which they had received on landing, and would not venture to follow.

But before morning the news of the evasion would spread far and wide, and there would be a hot pursuit among the mountains.

Scarce a word had been spoken in the boat. Marjory was pale and agitated, and Archie thought it best to leave her to herself. On the way through the wood he kept beside her, assisting her over rough places, and occasionally saying a few encouraging words. When darkness had completely set in three or four torches were lit, and they continued their way until midnight. Several times Archie had proposed a halt, but Marjory insisted that she was perfectly able to continue her way for some time longer.

At midnight, however, he halted.

"We will stop here," he said. "My men have been marching ever since daybreak, and t. morrow we must journey fast and far. I propose that we keep due east for some time and then along by Loch Rannoch, then across the Grampians by the pass of Killiecrankie, when we can make down to Perth, and so to Stirling. The news of your escape will fly fast to the south, and the tracks to Tarbert and the Clyde will all be watched; but if we start at daybreak we shall be far on our way east before they begin to search the hills here; and even if they think of our making in this direction, we shall be at Killiecrankie before they can cut us off."

CHAPTER XX.

THE HEIRESS OF THE KERRS.

WHILE Archie was speaking Marjory had sat down on a fallen tree. She had not slept the night before, and had been anxious and agitated the whole day. The excitement had kept her up; but she now felt completely worn out, and accepted without protest Archie's decision that a halt must be made.

The men were already gathering sticks, and a bright fire soon blazed near the spot where she had seated herself. Ere long some venison steaks were broiled in the flames. At Archie's earnest request Marjory tried to eat, but could with difficulty swallow a few morsels. A bower of green boughs was quickly made for her, and the ground thickly piled with fresh bracken, and Marjory was in a very few minutes sound asleep after the fatigue and excitement of the day.

With the first dawn of morning the men were on their feet. Fresh sticks were thrown on the fire and breakfast prepared, for the march would be a long and wearisome one.

"Breakfast is ready, Mistress Marjory,' Archie said, approaching the bower.

"And I am ready too," the girl said blithely as she appeared at the entrance. "The sleep has done wonders for me, and I feel brave and fresh again. I fear you must have thought me a terrible coward yesterday; but it all seemed so dreadful, such a wild and wicked thing to do, that I felt quite overwhelmed. To-day you will find me ready for anything."

"I could never think you a coward," Archie said, "after you faced the anger of that terrible uncle of yours for my sake; or rather," he added, "for the sake of your word. And now I hope you will eat something, for we have a long march through the forest and hills before us."

"Don't fear that I shall tire," she said. "I am half a mountaineer myself, and, methinks, can keep on my feet as long as any man."

The meal was hastily eaten, and then the party started on their way.

"I have been wondering," the girl said, as with light steps she kept pace with Archie's longer stride, "how you came to know that I was in the convert."

Archie looked surprised.

"How should I know, Mistress Marjory, but through your own messenger?"

"My own messenger!" Marjory exclaimed. "You are jesting, Sir Archie."

"I am not so, fair lady," he said. "Surely you must remember that you sent a messenger to me, with word that you were captive at St. Kenneth and needed my aid?"

The girl stopped for a moment in her walk and gazed at her companion as if to assure herself that he was in earnest. "You must be surely dreaming, Sir Archie," she said, as she continued the walk, "for assuredly I sent you no such message."

"But, lady," Archie said, holding out his hand, "the messenger brought me as token that he had come from you this ring which I had given you, vowing that should you call me to your aid I would come immediately, even from a stricken field."

The blood had rushed into the girl's face as she saw the ring. Then she turned very pale. "Sir Archibald Forbes," she said in a low tone, after walking for a minute or two in silence, "I feel disgraced in your eyes. How forward and unmaidenly must you have thought me thus to take advantage of a vow made from the impulse of sudden gratitude."

"No, indeed, lady," Archie said hotly. "No such thought ever entered my mind. I should as soon doubt the holy Virgin herself as to deem you capable of aught but what was sweet and womanly. The matter seemed to me simple enough. You had saved my life at great peril to yourself, and it seemed but natural to me that in your trouble, having none others to befriend you, your thoughts should turn to one who had sworn to be to the end of his life your faithful knight and servant. But," he went on more lightly, "since you yourself did not send me the ring and message, what good fairy can have brought them to me?"

"The good fairy was a very bad one," the girl said shortly, "and I will rate him soundly when I see him for thus adventuring without my consent. It is none other than Father Anselm; and yet," she added, "he has suffered so much on my behalf that I shall have to forgive him. After your escape my uncle in his passion was well-nigh hanging the good priest in spite of his holy office, and drove him from the castle. He kept me shut up in my room for many weeks, and then urged upon me the marriage with his son. When he found that I would not listen to it he sent me to St. Kenneth, and there I have remained ever since. Three weeks ago Father Anselm came to see me. He had been sent for by Alexander of Lorne, who, knowing the influence he had with me, begged him to undertake the mission of inducing me to bend to his will. As he knew how much I hated John of Lorne, the good priest wasted not much time in entreaties; but he warned me that it had been resolved that unless I gave way my captivity, which had hitherto been easy and pleasant, would be made hard and rigorous, and that I would be forced into accepting John of Lorne as a husband. When he saw that I was determined not to give in, the good priest certainly hinted" (and here she colored again hotly) "that you would, if sent for, do your best to carry me off. Of course I refused to listen to the idea, and chided him for suggesting so unmaidenly a course. He urged it no further, and I thought no more of the matter. The next day I missed my ring, which, to avoid notice,

I had worn on a little ribbon round my neck. I
thought at the time the ribbon must have broken
and the ring been lost, and for a time I made dili-
gent search in the garden for it; but I doubt not
now that the traitor priest, as I knelt before him to
receive his blessing on parting, must have severed the
ribbon and stolen it."

"God bless him!" Archie said fervently. "Should
he ever come to Aberfilly the warmest corner by
the fire, the fattest capon, and the best stoop of
wine from the cellar shall be his so long as he lives.
Why, but for him, Lady Marjory, you might have
worn out months of your life in prison, and have
been compelled at last to wed your cousin. I should
have been a miserable man for life."

The girl laughed.

"I would have given you a week, Sir Archie, and
no more; that is the extreme time which a knight
in our days can be expected to mourn for the fairest
lady; and now," she went on, changing the subject,
"think you we shall reach the pass across the Grampians before night?"

"If all goes well, lady, and your feet will carry
you so far, we shall be there by eventide. Unless
by some chance encounter we need have no fear
whatever of pursuit. It will have been daylight
before the news of your flight fairly spreads through
the country, though, doubtless, messengers were
sent off at once in all directions; but it would need
an army to scour these woods, and as they know
not whether we have gone east, west, north, or

south, the chance is faint indeed of any party meet
ing us, especially as we have taken so straight a line
that they must march without a pause in exactly the
right direction to come up with us."

At nightfall the party camped again on the slope
of the Grampians, and the following morning
crossed by the pass of Killiecrankie and made
toward Perth.

The next night Marjory slept in a peasant's
cottage, Archie and his companions lying down
without. Wishing to avoid attention, Archie purchased from the peasant the Sunday clothes of his
daughter, who was about the same age and size as
Marjory.

When they reached Perth he bought a strong
horse, with saddle and pillion; and with Marjory
behind him, and his band accompanying him on
foot, he rode for Stirling. When he neared the
town he heard that the king was in the forest of
Falkirk, and having consulted Marjory as to her
wishes rode directly thither.

Bruce, with his followers, had arrived but the
day before, and had taken up his abode at the
principal house of a village in the forest. He
came to the door when he heard the trampling of a
horse.

"Ah! Sir Archie, is it you safely returned, and,
as I half expected, a lady?"

"This, sire," Archie said, dismounting, "is Mistress Marjory MacDougall, of whom, as you have
heard me say, I am the devoted knight and servant.

She has been put in duress by Alexander of Lorne because in the first place she was a true Scots-woman and favored your cause, and because in the second place she refused to espouse his son John. I have borne her away from the convent of St. Kenneth, and as I used no force in doing so no sacrilege has been committed. I have brought her to you in all honor and courtesy, as I might a dear sister, and I now pray you to place her under the protection of the wife of one of your knights, seeing that she has no friends and natural protectors here. Then, when she has time to think, she must herself decide upon her future."

The king assisted Marjory to dismount.

"Fair mistress," he said, "Sir Archibald Forbes is one of the bravest and truest of my knights, and in the hands of none might you more confidingly place your honor. Assuredly I will do as he asks me, and will place you under the protection of Dame Elizabeth Graham, who is now within, having ridden hither to see her husband but this morning. But I trust," he added, with a meaning smile, "that you will not long require her protection."

The king entered the house with Marjory, while Archie, with his band, rejoined the rest of his party, who were still with the king. After having seen that the wants of those who had accompanied him had been supplied he returned to the royal quarters. The king met him at the door, and said, with a merry smile on his face:

"I fear me, Sir Archie, that all my good advice with regard to Mistress Mary Kerr has been wasted, and that you are resolved to make this Highland damsel, the niece of my arch-enemy Alexander of Lorne, your wife."

"If she will have me," Archie said stoutly, "such assuredly, is my intent; but of that I know nothing, seeing that, while she was under my protection, it would have been dishonorable to have spoken of love; and I know nought of her sentiments toward me, especially seeing that she herself did not, as I had hoped, send for me to come to her aid, and was indeed mightily indignant that another should have done so in her name."

"Poor Sir Archie!" the king laughed. "Though a man, and a valorous one in stature and in years, you are truly but a boy yet in these matters. It needed but half an eye to see by the way she turned pale and red when you spoke to her that she loves you. Now look you, Sir Archie," he went on more seriously; "these are troubled days, and one knows not what a day may bring forth. Graham's tower is neither strong nor safe, and the sooner this Mistress Marjory of yours is safely in your stronghold of Aberfilly the better for both of you, and for me also, for I know that you will be of no more good to me so long as your brain is running on her. Look you now, she is no longer under your protection, and your scruples on that head are therefore removed; best go in at once and ask her whether she will have you. If she says Yes, we will ride to Glasgow to-morrow or next day. The bishop shall marry you, and I myself will give you your bonny bride. This is no time for wasting weeks with milliners and mantua-makers. What say you?"

"Nothing would more surely suit my wishes, sire," Archie said; "but I fear she will think me presumptuous."

"Not a bit of it," the king laughed. "Highland lassies are accustomed to sudden wooing, and I doubt not that when she freed you last autumn from Dunstaffnage her mind was just as much made up as yours is as to the state of her heart. Come along, sir."

So saying, the king passed his arm through that of Archie, and drew him into the house. In the room which they entered Marjory was sitting with Lady Graham. Both rose as the king entered.

"My Lady Graham," the king said, "this my good and faithful knight Sir Archie Forbes, whose person as well as repute is favorably known to you, desires to speak alone with the young lady under your protection. I may say he does so at my special begging, seeing that at times like these the sooner matters are put in a straight course the better. Will you let me lead you to the next room while we leave the young people together?"

"Marjory," Archie said, when he and the girl were alone, "I fear that you will think my wooing rude and hasty, but the times must excuse it. I would fain have waited that you might have seen

more of me before I tried my fate; but in these
troubled days who can say where I may be a week
hence, or when I can see you again were I once
separated from you! Therefore, dear, I speak at
once. I love you, Marjory, and since the day when
you came like an angel into my cell at Dunstaffnage I have known that I loved you, and should I
never see you again could love none other. Will
you wed me, love?"

"But the king tells me, Sir Archie," the girl
said, looking up with a half smile, "that he wishes
you to wed the Lady Mary Kerr."

"It is a dream of the good king," Archie said,
laughing, "and he is not in earnest about it. He
knows that I have never set eyes on the lady or she
on me, and he was but jesting when he said so to
you, having known from me long ago that my
heart was wholly yours."

"Besides," the girl said, hesitating, "you might
have objected to wed Mistress Kerr because her
father was an enemy of yours."

"Why dwell upon it?" Archie said a little impa-
tiently. "Mistress Kerr is nothing in the world to
me, and I had clean forgotten her very existence,
when by some freak or other she sent her retainers
to fight under my command. She may be a sweet
and good lady for what I know; she may be the
reverse. To me she is absolutely nothing; and
now, Marjory, give me my answer. I love you,
dear, deeply and truly; and should you say Yes,
will strive all my life to make you happy."

"One more question, Archie, and then I will answer yours. Tell me frankly, had I been Mary Kerr instead of Marjory MacDougall, could you so far forget the ancient feud between the families as to say to me, I love you?"

Archie laughed.

"The question is easily answered. Were you your own dear self it would matter nought to me were your name Kerr, or MacDougall, or Comyn, or aught else. It is you I love, and your ancestors or your relations matter to me not one single jot."

"Then I will answer you," the girl said, putting her hands in his. "Archie Forbes, I love you with my whole heart, and have done so since I first met you; but," she said, drawing back, as Archie would have clasped her in his arms, "I must tell you that you have been mistaken, and that it is not Marjory MacDougall whom you would wed, but Mary, whom her uncle Alexander always called Marjory, Kerr."

"Marjory Kerr!" Archie repeated in astonishment.

"Yes, Archie, Marjory or Mary Kerr. The mistake was none of my making; it was you called me MacDougall; and knowing that you had reason to hate my race I did not undeceive you, thinking you might even refuse the boon of life at the hands of a Kerr. But I believed that when you thought it over afterward you would suspect the truth, seeing that it must assuredly come to your ears if you spoke of your adventure, even if you did not already know it, that Sir John Kerr and Alexander ot Lorne married twin sisters of the house of Comyn. You are not angry, I hope, Archie?"

"Angry!" Archie said, taking the girl, who now yielded unresistingly, in his arms. "It matters nothing to me who you were; and truly I am glad that the long feud between our houses will come to an end. My conscience, too, pricked me somewhat when I heard that by the death of your brother you had succeeded to the estates, and that it was in despite of a woman, and she a loyal and true-hearted Scotswoman, that I was holding Aberfilly. So it was you sent the retainers from Ayr to me?"

"Yes," Marjory replied. "Father Anselm carried my orders to them. I longed to know that they were fighting for Scotland, and was sure that under none could they be better led."

"And you have told the king who you are?" Archie asked.

"Yes," the girl said, "directly we entered."

"And you agree that we shall be married at once at Glasgow, as the king has suggested to me?"

"The king said as much to me," Marjory said, coloring; "but oh! Archie, it seems dreadful, such an unseemly bustle and haste, to be betrothed one day and married the next! Whoever heard of such a thing?"

"But the circumstances, Marjory, are exceptional. We all carry our lives in our hands, and things must be done which at another time would seem strange. Besides, what advantage would there be in waiting?

I should be away fighting the English and you would see no more of me. You would not get to know me better than you do now."

"Oh! it is not that, Archie."

"Nor is it anything else," Archie said, smiling, "but just surprise. With the King of Scotland to give you away and the Bishop of Glasgow to marry you, none can venture to hint that there is anything that is not in the highest degree orthodox in your marriage. Of course I shall have to be a great deal away until the war is over and Scotland freed of her tyrants. But I shall know that you are safe at Aberfilly, which is quite secure from any sudden attack. You will have my mother there to pet you and look after you in my absence, and I hope that good Father Anselm will soon find his way there and take up his abode. It is the least he can do, seeing that, after all, he is responsible for our marriage, and having, as it were, delivered you into my hands, ought to do his best to make you happy in your captivity."

Marjory raised no further objection. She saw, in truth, that, having once accepted Archie Forbes as her husband, it was in every way the best plan for her to marry him without delay, since she had no natural protectors to go to, and her powerful relations might stir up the church to view her evasion from the convent as a defiance of its authority.

Upon the following day the king moved with his force to Glasgow, which had already been evacuated by the English garrison, and the next morning Mar-

jory—for Archie through life insisted upon calling
her by the pet name under which he had first known
her—was married to Sir Archibald Forbes. The
Bruce gave her away, and presented her with a
splendid necklet of pearls. His brother Edward,
Sir James Douglas, and other companions of Archie
in the field also made the bride handsome presents.
Archie's followers from Aberfilly and the contin-
gent from Marjory's estates in Ayr were also present, together with a crowd of the townspeople, for
Archie Forbes, the companion of Wallace, was one
of the most popular characters in Scotland, and the
good city of Glasgow made a fête of his marriage.

Suddenly, as it was arranged, a number of the
daughters of the wealthiest citizens attired in white
attended the bride in procession to the altar. Flowers
were strewn and the bride and bridegroom were
heartily cheered by a concourse of people as they
left the cathedral.

The party then mounted, and the king, his brother,
Sir James Douglas, and some other knights, together with a strong escort, rode with them to
Aberfilly. Archie had despatched a messenger to
his mother with the news directly the arrangements
had been made ; and all was prepared for their
coming. The tenants had assembled to give a
hearty welcome to their lord and new mistress.
Dame Forbes received her as she alighted from the
pillion on which she had ridden behind Archie, and
embraced her tenderly.

It was the dearest wish of her life that Archie

should marry; and, although when she first heard
the news, she regretted in her heart that he should
have chosen a Kerr, still she saw that the union
would put an end to the long feud, and might even,
in the event of the final defeat of Bruce, be the
means of safety for Archie himself and security for
his possessions.

She soon, however, learned to love Marjory for
herself, and to be contented every way with her
son's choice. There was high feasting and revelry
at Aberfilly that evening. Bonfires were burned in
the castle yard, and the tenants feasted there, while
the king and his knights were entertained in the
hall of the castle.

The next morning the king and his companions
again mounted and rode off. Sir James Douglas
was going south to harry Galloway and to revenge
the assaults which the people had made upon the
king. There was a strong English force there
under Sir Ingram Umfraville and Sir John de St.
John.

"I will give you a week, Sir Archie, to take
holiday, but can spare you no longer. We have as
yet scarce begun our work, for well-nigh every
fortress in Scotland is in English hands, and we
must take as many of them as we can before
Edward moves across the border again."

"I will not outstay the time," Sir Archie said.
"As we arranged last night, I will march this day
week with my retainers to join Sir James Douglas
in Galloway."

CHAPTER XXI.

THE SIEGE OF ABERFILLY.

PUNCTUAL to his agreement Archie Forbes marched south with his retainers. He was loath, indeed, to leave Marjory, but he knew well that a long time indeed must elapse before he could hope to settle down quietly at home, and that it was urgent to hurry on the work at once before the English made another great effort to stamp out the movement. Marjory did not attempt to induce him to overstay his time. She was too proud of his position as one of the foremost knights of Scotland to say a word to detain him from the field. So she bade him adieu with a brave face, reserving her tears until after he had ridden away.

It had been arranged that Archie should operate independently of Douglas, the two joining their forces only when threatened by overwhelming numbers or when any great enterprise was to be undertaken. Archie took with him a hundred and fifty men from his estates in Lanark and Ayr. He marched first to Loudon Hill, then down through Cumnock and the border of Carrick into Galloway. Contrary to the usual custom, he enjoined his retainers on no account to burn or harry the villages and granges.

"The people," he said, "are not responsible for the conduct of their lords, and as I would not see the English harrying the country round Aberfilly, so I am loath to carry fire and sword among these poor people. We have come hither to punish their lords and to capture their castles. If the country people oppose us we must needs fight them; but beyond what is necessary for our provision let us take nothing from them, and show them, by our conduct, that we hold them to be Scotchmen like ourselves, and that we pity rather than blame them, inasmuch as by the orders of their lords they are forced to fight against us."

Archie had not advanced more than a day's march into Galloway when he heard that Sir John de St. John was marching with four hundred men-at-arms to meet him.

There were no better soldiers in the following of Bruce than the retainers of Aberfilly and Glen Cairn. They had now for many years been frequently under arms, and were thoroughly trained to fight together. They had the greatest confidence in themselves and their leader, and having often with their spears withstood the shock of the English chivalry, Archie knew that he could rely upon them to the fullest. He therefore took up a position on the banks of a river where a ford would enable the enemy to cross. Had he been less confident as to the result he would have defended the ford, which could be only crossed by two horsemen abreast. He determined, however, to repeat the maneuver which had proved so successful at Stirling Bridge, and to let half of the enemy cross before he fell upon them.

The ground near the river was stony and rough. Great boulders, which had rolled from the hillside, were thickly scattered about it, and it would be difficult for cavalry to charge up the somewhat steeply sloping ground in anything like unbroken order.

With eighty of his men Archie took up a position one hundred yards back from the stream. With great exertions some of the smaller boulders were removed, and with rocks and stones were piled to make a wall on either flank of the ground, which, standing two deep, he occupied. The remaining seventy men he divided equally, placing one company under the command of each of his two faithful lieutenants, Andrew Macpherson and William Orr. These took post near the river, one on each side of the ford, and at a distance of about one hundred yards therefrom. Orr's company were hidden among some bushes growing by the river. Macpherson's lay down among the stones and boulders, and were scarce likely to attract the attention of the English, which would naturally be fixed upon the little body drawn up to oppose them in front. The preparations were scarcely completed when the English were seen approaching. They made no halt at the river, but at once commenced crossing at the ford, confident in their power to overwhelm the

little body of Scots, whose number had, it seemed
to them, been exaggerated by the fears of the
country people. As soon as a hundred of the men-
at-arms had passed, their leader marshaled them in
line, and with level spears charged up the slopes
against Archie's force. The great boulders broke
their ranks, and it was but in straggling order that
they reached the narrow line of Scottish spears.

These they in vain endeavored to break through.
Their numbers were of no avail to them, as, being
on horseback, but twenty men at a time could attack
the double row of spearmen. While the conflict
was at its height Archie's trumpet was sounded, for
he saw that another hundred men had now crossed
the ford.

At the signal the two hidden parties leaped to
their feet, and with leveled pikes rushed toward the
ford. The English had no force there to resist the
attack, for as the men-at-arms had passed, each had
ridden on to join the fray in front. The head of
the ford was therefore seized with but little difficulty. Orr, with twenty men, remained here to
hold it and prevent others from crossing, while
Macpherson, with fifty, ran up the hill and fell
upon the rear of the confused mass of cavalry, who
were striving in vain to break the line of Archie's
spears.

The attack was decisive; the English, surprised
and confused by the sudden attack, were unable to
offer any effectual resistance to Macpherson's pikemen, and at the same moment that these fell upon

the rear, Archie gave the word and his men rushed forward upon the struggling mass of cavalry. The shock was irresistible ; men and horses fell in numbers under the Scottish spears, and in a few minutes those who could manage to extricate themselves from the struggling mass rode off in various directions. These, however, were few in number, for ninety were killed and seventy taken prisoners. St. John himself succeeded in cutting his way through the spearmen, and, swimming the river below the ford, rejoined his followers, who had in vain endeavored to force the passage of the ford. With these he rapidly retired.

A detachment of fifty men were sent off with the prisoners to Bruce, and Archie with the main body of his followers, two days later joined the force under Sir James Douglas.

Upon the following morning a messenger from Aberfilly reached Archie.

" My lord," he said, " I bring you a message from the Lady Marjory. I have spent five days in searching for you, and have never but once laid down during that time, therefore do not blame me if my message is long in coming."

" What is it, Evan ? naught is wrong there, I trust ?"

" The Lady Marjory bade me tell you that news has reached her, that from each of the garrisons of Ayr, Lanark, Stirling, and Bothwell, a force is marching toward your hold, which the governor of Bothwell has sworn to destroy. When I left they were expected hourly in sight, and this is full a week since."

"Aberfilly can hold out for longer than that," Archie said, "against aught but surprise, and the vassals would have had time to gather."

"Yes," the man replied, "they were flocking in when I came away; the men of Glen Cairn had already arrived; all the women and children were taking to the hills, according to the orders which you gave."

"And now, good Evan, do you eat some supper, and then rest. No wonder you have been so long in finding me, for I have been wandering without ceasing. I will start at once with my followers here for Aberfilly; by to-morrow evening we will be there."

Archie hurried to the hut occupied by Douglas, told him the news, and said he must hurry away to the defense of his castle.

"Go, by all means, Archie," Douglas replied. "If I can gather a force sufficient to relieve you I will myself march thither; but at present I fear that the chances of my doing so are small, for the four garrisons you have named would be able to spare a force vastly larger than any with which I could meet them in the field, and the king is no better able to help you."

"I will do my best," Archie said. "The castle can stand a stout siege; and fortunately I have a secret passage by which we can escape."

"Never mind the castle," Douglas replied.

"When better days come we will rebuild it again for you."

A few notes on a horn brought Archie's little band of followers together. Telling them the danger which threatened Glen Clairn, Archie placed himself at their head, and at a rapid step they marched away. It was five-and-forty miles across the hills, but before morning they approached it, and made their way to the wood in which was the entrance to the subterranean passage leading to the castle. Archie had feared that they might find the massive doors which closed it, a short distance from the entrance, securely fastened as usual. They were shut, indeed, but as they approached them they heard a challenge from within.

"It is I, Sir Archie Forbes."

The door was opened at once. "Welcome, Sir Archie!" the guard said. "The Lady Marjory has been expecting you for the last five days, and a watch has been kept here constantly, to open the doors should you come."

"The messenger could not find me," Archie said. "Is all well at the castle?"

"All is well," the man replied. "The English have made two attacks, but have been beaten back with loss. This morning some great machines have arrived from Stirling and have begun battering the walls. Is it your will that I remain here on guard, now that you have come?"

"Yes," Archie answered. "It were best that one should be always stationed here, seeing that the entrance might perchance be discovered by one wandering in the wood, or they might obtain the secret of its existence from a prisoner. If footsteps are heard approaching retire at once with the news. There is no danger if we are warned in time, for we can turn the water from the moat into it."

Archie and his followers now made their way along the passage until they entered the castle. As they issued out from the entrance a shout of joy rose from those near, and the news rapidly flew through the castle that Archie had arrived. In a moment Marjory ran down and threw herself into his arms.

"Welcome back, Archie, a thousand times! I have been grievously anxious as the days went on and you did not return, and had feared that some evil must have befallen you. It has been a greater anxiety to me than the defense of the castle; but I have done my best to be hopeful and bright, to keep up the spirits of our followers."

"It was no easy task for your messenger to find me, Marjory, for we are ever on the move. Is my mother here?"

"No, Archie, she went a fortnight since on a visit to Lady Gordon."

"It is well," Archie said, "for if in the end we have to leave the castle, you, who have proved yourself so strong and brave, can, if needs be, take to the hills with me; but she could not support the fatigues of such a life. And now, dear, we have marched all night and shall be glad of food; while it is preparing I will to the walls and see what is going on."

As Archie reached the battlement a loud cheer broke from the defenders gathered there, and Sandy Grahame hurried up to him.

"Welcome back, Sir Archie; glad am I to give up the responsibility of this post, although, indeed, it is not I who have been in command, but Lady Marjory. She has been always on the walls, cheering the men with her words and urging them to deeds of bravery; and, indeed, she has frightened me sorely by the way in which she exposed herself where the arrows were flying most thickly, for as I told her over and over again, if the castle were taken I knew that you would be sure that I had done my best, but what excuse should I be able to make to you if I had to bear you the news that she had been killed?"

"And what did she say to that, Sandy?"

"Truth, Sir Archie, she's a woman and willful, and she just laughed and said that you would know you could not keep her in order yourself, and could not therefore expect me to rule her."

"That is so, Sandy," Archie laughed; "but now that I am back I will for once exert my authority, and will see that she runs into no further danger. And now, how goes the siege?"

"So far they have done but little damage, Sir Archie; but the machines which they brought up yesterday will, I fear, play havoc with our walls.

They have not yet begun their work, for when they brought them up yesterday afternoon our men shot so hotly that they had to fall back again; but in the night they have thrown up high banks of earth, and have planted the engines under their shelter, and will, ere long, begin to send their messengers against our walls. Thrice they assaulted the works beyond the drawbridge and twice we beat them back; but last night they came on with all their force. I was myself there, and after fighting for awhile and seeing they were too strong for us, I thought it best to withdraw before they gained footing in the work, and so had time to draw off the men and raise the drawbridge."

"Quite right, Sandy! The defenders of the post would only have been slaughtered, and the assailants might have rushed across the drawbridge before it could have been raised. The post is of little importance save to defend the castle against a sudden surprise, and would only have been a source of constant anxiety and loss. How many do you reckon them? Judging by their tents there must be three or four thousand."

"About three thousand, Sir Archie, I make it; and as we had no time to get the tenants in from my lady's Ayrshire estate, we have but two hundred men in the castle, and many of these are scarce more than boys."

"I have brought a hundred and fifty with me, Sandy, so we have as many as we can use on the walls, though I could wish I had another hundred or two for sorties."

Half an hour later the great machines began to work, hurling vast stones with tremendous force against the castle wall. Strongly as this was built, Archie saw that it would ere many days crumble before the blows.

"I did not reckon on such machines as these," he said to Sandy. "Doubtless they are some of the huge machines which King Edward had constructed for the siege of Stirling, and which have remained there since the castle was taken. Fortunately we have still the moat when a breach is made, and it will be hard work to cross that."

All day the great stones thundered against the wall. The defenders were not idle, but kept up a shower of arrows at the edge of the mound behind which the machines were hidden; but although many of those working there were killed, fresh relays came constantly up, and the machines never ceased their work. By nightfall the face of the wall was bruised and battered. Many of the stones in front had fallen from their places.

"Another twenty-four hours," Archie said to Marjory, as he joined her in the great hall, "and the breach will be begun, forty-eight and it will be completed. They will go on all night, and we may expect no rest until the work is done. In an hour's time I shall sally out from the passage into the wood and beat up their camp. Expecting no attack from the rear, we shall do them rare damage ere they can gather to oppose us. As soon as they do so we shall be off again, and, scattering in various directions, gather again in the wood and return here."

An hour later Archie, with two hundred men, started. No sooner had he left than Marjory called Sandy Grahame and Andrew Macpherson, whom he had left in joint command during his absence.

" Now," she said, " I am not going to remain quiet here while Sir Archie does all the fighting, therefore do you gather all the garrison together, leaving only twenty to hold the gate. See that the wheels of the drawbridge are well oiled, and the hinges of the gate. Directly we see that the attack has begun upon the camp we will lower the draw- bridge quietly, open the gates, and sally out. There is no great force in the outer work. When we have cleared that—which, if we are quick, we can do without alarming the camp, seeing what a confusion and uproar will be going on there—we will make straight along to the point where the machines are placed. Let some of the men take axes and cut the ropes, and let others carry fagots well steeped in oil, we will pile them round the machines and light them, and thus having ensured their destruction, we will fall back again."

" But, Lady Marjory—" Sandy began.

" I will have no buts, Sandy ; you must just do as I order you, and I will answer to Sir Archie. I shall myself go forth with you and see that the work is properly done."

The two men looked doubtfully at each other.

" Now, Andrew," Marjory said briskly, " let us have no hesitation or talk, the plan is a good one."

"I do not say that it is not a good one," Sandy replied cautiously, "or that it is not one that Sir Archie might have carried out if he had been here."

"Very well, Andrew, then that is quite enough. I give you the orders and I am responsible, and if you and Sandy do not choose to obey me, I shall call the men together myself and lead them without you."

As Sandy and Andrew were quite conscious that their lady would be as good as her word, they at once proceeded to carry her orders into effect. The wheels of the portcullis and drawbridge were oiled, as were the bolts and hinges of the gate. The men were formed up in the courtyard, where presently they were joined by Marjory who had put on a light steel cap and a shirt of mail, and who had armed herself with a light sword. The men gathered round her enthusiastically, and would have burst into cheers had she not held up her hand to command silence.

"I will to the wall now," she said, "to watch for the signal. The instant the attack begins and the attention of those in the outwork is called that way, draw up the portcullis noiselessly and open the gate, oil the hinges of the drawbridge and have everything in readiness; then I will join you. Let the draw bridge be lowered swiftly, and as it falls we will rush across. You have, I suppose, told off the men who are to remain behind. Tell them that when the last of us have crossed they are to raise the drawbridge a few feet, so that none can cross it until we return."

Then, accompanied by Macpherson, she ascended the walls. All was quiet in the hostile camp, which was about a quarter of a mile distant, and only the creaking of the wheels of the machines, the orders of those directing them, and the dull crash as the great stones struck the wall, broke the stillness of the night. For half an hour they watched, and then a sudden uproar was heard in the camp. The Scottish war-cry pealed out, followed by shouts and yells, and almost instantly flames were seen to mount up.

"My lord is at work," Marjory said, "it is time for us to be doing also." So saying she ran down to the courtyard. Sandy Grahame, Macpherson, and a few picked men took their place around her, then the drawbridge was suddenly run down, and the Scots dashed across it. As Marjory had anticipated, the English in the outwork had gathered on the further side and were watching the sudden outbreak in the camp. Alarmed at the prospect of an attack, perhaps by the Bruce, in that quarter, they were suddenly startled by the rush of feet across the drawbridge, and before they had time to recover from their surprise the Scots were upon them. The latter were superior in numbers, and the English, already alarmed by the attack upon their camp, offered but a feeble resistance. Many were cut down, but the greater part leaped from the wall and fled toward the camp. The moment resistance ceased the outer gate was thrown open, and at full speed the Scotch made for the machines. The party here had suspended their work and were gazing toward the camp, where the uproar was now great. The wind was blowing briskly and the fire had spread with immense rapidity, and already half the camp was in flames. Suddenly from the bank above the Scots poured down upon them like a torrent. There was scarcely a thought of resistance. Stricken with dismay and astonishment at this unexpected attack the soldiers working the machines fled hastily, only a few falling beneath the swords of the Scots. The men with axes at once fell upon the machines, cutting the ropes and smashing the wheels and levers which worked them, while those with the fagots piled them round. In less than two minutes the work was done, lighted torches were applied to the fagots, and the flames soon shot up hotly.

The Scots waited but a minute or two to see that the work was thoroughly done and that the flames had got fair hold, and then, keeping in a close body, they retired to the castle. Not a soul was met with by the way, and leaving Andrew Macpherson with fifty men to hold the outwork until Archie should return and decide whether it should be occupied, Marjory, with the rest, re-entered the castle.

She at once ascended to the walls again, where Sandy also posted the men to be in readiness to open fire with their arrows should the English return and endeavor to extinguish the flames round the machines. The sound of fighting had ceased at the camp. By the light of the flames numbers of the English could be seen pulling down the tents which the fire had not yet reached and endeavoring to check the conflagration, while a large body of horse and foot were rapidly advancing toward the castle.

As soon as they came within bowshot range the archers opened fire, and the English leaders, seeing that it was already too late to save the machines, which were by this time completely enveloped in flames, and that men would only be sacrificed to no good purpose, halted the troops. They then moved toward the outwork, but finding this in possession of the Scots, they fell back again to the camp to take council as to the next steps to be adopted.

Archie's attack had been crowned with complete success. Apprehending no danger from behind, the English had neglected to place sentries there, and the Scots were already among the tents before their presence was discovered. Numbers of the English were cut down and the tents fired, and as soon as the English recovered from their first surprise and began to form, Archie gave the word for a retreat. This was effected without molestation, for the first thought of the English was to save the camp from total destruction. The reports of the men who escaped from the castle outwork and the outburst of flames around the machines added to the confusion which reigned, and the leaders, who had by the light of the flames ascertained that the assault upon the camp had been made by a small body of the enemy, deemed it of the first importance to move at once to save the machines if it were still possible.

The Scots regained the entrance to the passage without the loss of a single man, and passing through, soon re-entered the castle. Marjory had laid aside her warlike trappings and awaited her husband's return at the inner entrance of the passage.

" We have had good success, Marjory," Archie said as he greeted her, " as you will have seen from the walls. The greater part of the English camp is destroyed; we have killed great numbers, and have not lost a man."

"That is good news indeed, Archie. We, too, have not been quite idle while you have been away."

"Why, what have you been doing, Marjory?" Archie asked in surprise.

" Come up to the walls and I will show you."

Archie mounted with her, and gave a start of surprise as he looked toward the machines. The great body of fire had died down now, but the beams of the machines stood up red and glowing, while a light flickering flame played round them.

" You see we have not been idle, Archie. We have destroyed the machines, and retaken the out-work, which is now held by Andrew Macpherson with fifty men."

" Why, what magic is this, wife?"

" No magic at all, sir knight. We have been carrying out the work which you, as a wise and skillful commander, should have ordered before you left. We have taken advantage of the confusion of the enemy by the fire in their camp, and have made a sortie, and a successful one, as you see."

"I am delighted, indeed," Archie said; "and the destruction of those machines is indeed a great work. Still Sandy and Macpherson should not have undertaken it without orders from me; they might have been cut off and the castle stormed before I came back."

"They had orders from me, sir, and that was quite sufficient. To do them justice, they hesitated about obeying me, and I was well-nigh ordering them to the dungeon for disobedience; and they only gave way at last when I said they could stop at home if they liked, but that I should lead out the retainers. Of course I went in your place, with armor and sword; but perhaps it was as well that I had no fighting to do."

"Do you mean, Marjory, that you really led the sortie?"

"I don't think I led it, Archie; but I certainly went out with it, and very exciting it was. There, dear, don't look troubled. Of course, as chatelaine of the castle, I was bound to animate my men."

"You have done bravely and well, indeed, Marjory, and I am proud of my wife. Still, dear, I tremble at the thought of the risk you ran."

"No more risk than you are constantly running, Archie; and I am rather glad you tremble, because in future you will understand my feelings better, left here all alone while you are risking your life perpetually with the king."

The success of the sally and the courage and energy shown by Marjory raised the spirits of the

garrison to the highest pitch; and had Archie
given the word they would have sallied out and
fallen upon the besiegers. Two days later fresh
machines arrived from Stirling, and the attack
again commenced, the besiegers keeping a large
body of men near the gate to prevent a repetition
of the last sally. Archie now despatched two or
three fleet-footed runners through the passage to
find the king, and tell him that the besiegers were
making progress, and to pray him to come to his
assistance. Two days passed, and the breach was
now fairly practicable, but the moat, fifty feet
wide, still barred the way to the besiegers. Archie
had noticed that for two or three days no water
had come down from above, and had no doubt that
they had diverted the course of the river. Upon
the day after the breach was completed the besiegers advanced in great force up the stream from
below.

"They are going to try to cut the dam," Archie
said to Sandy; "place every man who can draw a
bow on that side of the castle."

As the English approached a rain of arrows was
poured into them, but covering themselves with
their shields and with large mantlets formed of
hurdles covered with hides they pressed forward to
the dam. Here those who had brought with them
picks and mattocks set to work upon the dam, the
men with mantlets shielding them from the storm
of arrows, while numbers of archers opened fire
upon the defenders. Very many were killed by

The defense of Aberfilly Castle.—Page 367.

—*In Freedom's Cause.*

the Scottish arrows, but the work went on. A gap was made through the dam. The water, as it rushed through, aided the efforts of those at work; and after three hours' labor and fighting the gap was so far deepened that the water in the moat had fallen eight feet. Then, finding that this could now be waded, the assailants desisted, and drew off to their camp.

A council was held that evening in the castle as to whether the hold should be abandoned at once or whether one attack on the breach should be withstood. It was finally determined that the breach should be held. The steep sides of the moat, exposed by the subsidence of the water, were slippery and difficult. The force in the castle was amply sufficient at once to man the breach and to furnish archers for the walls on either side, while in the event of the worst, were the breach carried by the English, the defenders might fall back to the central keep, and thence make their way through the passage. Had it not been for the possibility of an early arrival of the king to their relief all agreed that it would be as well to evacuate the castle at once, as this in the end must fall, and every life spent in its defense would thus be a useless sacrifice. As, however, troops might at any moment appear, it was determined to hold the castle until the last.

The next morning a party of knights in full defensive armor came down to the edge of the moat to see whether a passage could be effected. They were not molested while making their examination, as the Scottish arrows would only have dropped harmless off their steel harness. Archie was on the walls.

"How like you the prospect, sir knights?" he called out merrily. "I fear that the sludge and slime will sully your bright armor and smirch your plumes, for it will be difficult to hold a footing on those muddy banks."

"It were best for you to yield, Sir Archibald Forbes, without giving us the trouble of making our way across your moat. You have made a stout resistance, and have done enough for honor, and you must see that sooner or later we must win our way in."

"Then I would rather it should be later," Archie replied. "I may have done enough for honor, but it is not for honor that I am fighting, but for Scotland. Your work is but begun yet, I can assure you. We are far from being at the end of our resources yet. It will be time enough to talk about surrendering when you have won the breach and the outer walls."

The knights retired; and as some hours passed without the besiegers seeing any preparation for an assault they judged that the report carried back to camp was not an encouraging one. Large numbers of men were, however, seen leaving the camp, and these toward sunset came back staggering under immense loads of brushwood which they had cut in the forest.

"They intend to fill up the moat," Archie said;
"it is their wisest course."

He at once directed his men to make up large
trusses of straw, over which he poured considerable
quantities of oil. Early the next morning the
English drew out of their camp, and advanced in
martial array. Each man carried a great fagot, and,
covering themselves with these as they came within
bowshot, they marched down to the moat. Each
in turn threw in his fagot, and when he had done
so returned to the camp and brought back another.
Rapidly the process of filling up the moat opposite
to the breach continued. The besiegers kept up a
rain of arrows and darts and many of the English
were killed. But the work was continued without
intermission until well-nigh across the moat a broad
crossway was formed level with the outer bank,
but a narrow gap remained to be filled, and the
English leaders advanced to the front to prevent
the Scots on the breach rushing down to assault
those placing the fagots.

Somewhat to the surprise of the English the
defenders remained stationary, contenting themselves with hurling great stones at their busy
enemy. Suddenly there was a movement. Archie
and a party of his best men dashed down the
breach, and, climbing on the causeway, for a
moment drove the workers and their guards back.
They were followed by twenty men carrying great
trusses of straw. These were piled against the
fagots forming the end of the causeway. Archie

and his band leaped back as a torch was applied to
the straw. In a moment the hot flames leaped up,
causing the knights who had pressed after the
retreating Scots to fall back hastily. A shout of
triumph rose from the garrison and one of dismay
from the besiegers. Saturated with oil, the trusses
burned with fury, and the fagots were soon alight.
A fresh wind was blowing, and the flames crept
rapidly along the causeway. In a few minutes this
was in a blaze from end to end, and in half an hour
nothing remained of the great pile save charred
ashes and the saturated fagots which had been
below the water in the moat, and which now floated
upon it.

The besiegers had drawn off when they saw that
the flames had gained a fair hold of the causeway.
The smoke had scarcely ceased to rise when a
great outcry arose from the English camp, and the
lookout from the top of the keep perceived a strong
force marching toward it. By the bustle and confusion which reigned in the camp Archie doubted
not that the newcomers were Scots. The garrison
were instantly called to arms. The gates were
thrown open, and leaving a small body only to
hold the gates, he sallied out at the head of his men
and marched toward the English camp.

At the approach of the Scottish force the English
leaders had marched out with their men to oppose
them. Bruce had been able to collect but three
hundred and fifty men, and the English, seeing how
small was the number advancing against them,

prepared to receive them boldly. Scarcely had the combat begun when Archie with his band entered the English camp, which was almost deserted. They at once fired the tents, and then advanced in a solid mass with level spears against the rear of the English. These, dismayed at the destruction of their camp, and at finding themselves attacked both front and rear, lost heart and fell into confusion. Their leaders strove to rally them, and dashed with their men-at arms against the spearmen, but their efforts to break through were in vain, and their defeat increased the panic of the footmen. Archie's party broke a way through their disordered line and joined the body commanded by the king, and the whole rushed so fiercely upon the English that these broke and fled in all directions, pursued by the triumphant Scots.

"I am but just in time I see, Sir Archie," Bruce said, pointing to the breach in the wall; "a few hours more and methinks that I should have been too late."

"We could have held out longer than that, sire," Archie replied. "We have repulsed an attack this morning and burned a causeway of fagots upon which they attempted to cross the moat; still, I am truly glad that you have arrived, and thank you with all my heart for coming so speedily to my rescue, for sooner or later the hold must have fallen; the great machines which they brought with them from Stirling proved too strong for the wall."

"And how has the Lady Marjory borne her during the siege?" the king inquired.

"Right nobly," Archie replied; "ever in good spirits and showing a brave face to the men; and one night when I made a sortie through my secret passage, and fell upon the English camp from the other side, having left the castle in her charge, she headed the garrison, and issuing out recaptured the outworks and destroyed the machines by fire."

"Bravely done," the king said, "and just what I should expect from your wife. You did well to take my advice in that matter."

"We shall never agree there, sire, for as you know I followed my own will and wed the bride I had fixed upon for myself."

"Well, well, Sir Archie, as we are both satisfied we will e'en let it be; and now, I trust that you have still some supplies left, for to tell you the truth I am hungry as well as weary, and my men have marched fast and far."

"There is an abundance," Archie replied, "to last them all for a month, and right willingly is it at their service."

The king remained a week at Aberfilly, his men aiding Archie's retainers in repairing the gap in the dam and in rebuilding the wall; and as five hundred men working willingly and well can effect wonders, by the time Bruce rode away the castle was restored to its former appearance. Archie marched on the following day and rejoined Douglas in Galloway

CHAPTER XXII.

A PRISONER.

AFTER some consultation between the leaders it was agreed to make an attempt to capture the castle of Knockbawn. It was known to possess a garrison of some sixty men only, and although strong, Archie and Sir James believed that it could be captured by assault. It was arranged that Archie should ride to reconnoiter it, and taking two mounted retainers he started, the force remaining in the forest some eight miles distant. The castle of Knockbawn stood on a rocky promontory, jutting a hundred and fifty yards into the sea. When he neared the neck of the point, which was but some twenty yards wide, Archie bade his followers fall back a short distance.

"I will ride," he said, "close up to the castle walls. My armor is good, and I care not for arrow or crossbow bolt. It were best you fell back a little, for they may have horses and may sally out in pursuit. I am well mounted and fear not being overtaken, but it were best that you should have a good start."

Archie then rode forward toward the castle.

Seeing a knight approaching alone the garrison
judged that he was friendly, and it was not until it
was seen that instead of approaching the drawbridge
he turned aside and rode to the edge of the fosse,
that they suspected that he was a foe.   Running to
the walls they opened fire with arrows upon him,
but by this time Archie had seen all that he required.
Across the promontory ran a sort of fissure, some
ten yards wide and as many deep.   From the opposite edge of this the wall rose abruptly.   Here assault would be difficult, and it was upon the gate-
way that an attack must be made.   Several arrows
had struck his armor and glanced off, and Archie
now turned and quietly rode away, his horse being
protected by mail like himself.   Scarce had he
turned when he saw a sight which caused him for
a moment to draw rein.   Coming at full gallop
toward the promontory was a strong body of English horse, flying the banner of Sir Ingram de Umfraville.   They were already nearer to the end of
the neck than he was.   There was no mode of escape, and drawing his sword he galloped at full
speed to meet them.   As he neared them Sir Ingram
himself, one of the doughtiest of Edward's knights,
rode out with leveled lance to meet him.   At full
gallop the knights charged each other.   Sir Ingram's
spear was pointed at the bars of Archie's helmet,
but as the horses met each other Archie with a blow
of his sword cut off the head of the lance and dealt
a tremendous backhanded blow upon Sir Ingram's
helmet as the latter passed him, striking the knight

forward on to his horse's neck; then without paus-
ing a moment he dashed into the midst of the
English ranks.

The horsemen closed around him, and although
he cut down several with his sweeping blows he was
unable to break his way through them. Such a conflict could not last long. Archie received a blow
from behind which struck him from his horse. Re-
gaining his feet he continued the fight, but the
blows rained thick upon him, and he was soon struck
senseless to the ground.

When he recovered he was in a room in the keep
of the castle. Two knights were sitting at a table
near the couch on which he was lying. "Ah!" exclaimed one, on seeing Archie open his eyes and
move, "I am glad to see your senses coming back to
you, sir prisoner. Truly, sir, I regret that so brave
a knight should have fallen into my hands, seeing
that in this war we must needs send our prisoners
to King Edward, whose treatment of them is not, I
must e'en own, gentle; for indeed you fought like
any paladin. I deemed not that there was a knight
in Scotland, save the Bruce himself, who could have
so borne himself; and never did I, Ingram de Umfraville, come nearer to losing my seat than I did
from that backhanded blow you dealt me. My
head rings with it still. My helmet will never be
fit to wear again, and as the leech said when plas-
tering my head, 'had not my skull been of the
thickest, you had assuredly cut through it.' May I
crave the name of so brave an antagonist?"

"I am Sir Archibald Forbes," Archie replied.

"By St. Jago!" the knight said, "but I am sorry for it, seeing that, save Bruce himself, there is none in the Scottish ranks against whom King Edward is so bitter. In the days of Wallace there was no one whose name was more often on our lips than that of Sir Archibald Forbes, and now, under Bruce, it is ever coming to the front. I had thought to have asked Edward as a boon that I should have kept you as my prisoner until exchanged for one on our side, but being Sir Archibald Forbes I know that it were useless indeed; nevertheless, sir knight, I will send to King Edward, begging him to look mercifully upon your case, seeing how bravely and honorably you have fought."

"Thanks for your good offices, Sir Ingram," Archie replied, "but I shall ask for no mercy for myself. I have never owed or paid him allegiance, but, as a true Scot, have fought for my country against a foreign enemy."

"But King Edward does not hold himself to be a foreign enemy," the knight said, "seeing that Baliol, your king, with Comyn and all your great nobles, did homage to him as lord-paramount of Scotland."

"It were an easy way," Archie rejoined, "to gain a possession, to nominate a puppet from among the nobles already your vassals, and then to get him to do homage. No, sir knight, neither Comyn nor Baliol, nor any other of the Anglo-Norman nobles who hold estates in Scotland, have a right to speak for her, or to barter away her freedom. That is

what Wallace and thousands of Scotchmen have
fought and died to protest against, and what Scotchmen will do until their country is free."

"It is not a question for me to argue upon," Sir
Ingram said surlily. " King Edward bids me fight
in Scotland, and as his knight and vassal I put on
my harness without question. But I own to you
that, seeing I have fought beside him in Gascony,
when he as a feudal vassal of the King of France
made war upon his lord, I cannot see that the
offense is an unpardonable one when you Scotchmen do the same here. Concerning the lawfulness
of his claim to be your lord-paramount, I own
that I neither know nor care one jot. However,
sir, I regret much that you have fallen into my
hands, for to Carlisle, where the king has long been
lying, as you have doubtless heard, grievously ill, I
must forthwith send you. I must leave you here
with the governor, for in half an hour I mount and
ride away with my troop. He will do his best to
make your sojourn here easy until such time as I
may have an opportunity of sending you by ship to
Carlisle; and now farewell, sir," he said, giving
Archie his hand, "I regret that an unkind chance
has thrown so gallant a knight into my hands, and
that my duty to the king forbids me from letting
you go free."

"Thanks, Sir Ingram," Archie replied. "I have
ever heard of you as a brave knight, and if this mis-
fortune must fall upon me, would sooner that I
should have been captured by you than by one of
less fame and honor."

The governor now had a meal with some wine set before Archie and then left him alone.

"I am not at Carlisle yet," Archie said to himself. "Unless I mistake, we shall have Sir James thundering at the gate before morning. Cluny will assuredly have ridden off at full speed to carry the news when he saw that I was cut off, and e'en now he will be marching toward the castle." As he expected, Archie was roused before morning by a tremendous outburst of noise. Heavy blows were given, followed by a crash, which Archie judged to be the fall of the drawbridge across the fosse. He guessed that some of Douglas' men had crept forward noiselessly, had descended the fosse, and managed to climb up to the gate, and had then suddenly attacked with their axes the chains of the drawbridge.

A prodigious uproar raged in the castle. Orders were shouted, and the garrison, aroused from their sleep, snatched up their arms and hastened to the walls. Outside rose the war-cry, "A Douglas! A Douglas!" mingled with others of, "Glen Cairn to the rescue!" For a few minutes all was confusion, then a light suddenly burst up and grew every instant more and more bright.

"Douglas has piled fagots against the gates," Archie said to himself. "Another quarter of an hour and the castle will be his."

Three or four minutes later the governor with six soldiers, two of whom bore torches, entered the room. "You must come along at once, sir knight," the governor said. "The attack is of the fiercest, and I know not whether we shall make head against it, but at any rate I must not risk your being recaptured, and must therefore place you in a boat and send you off without delay to the castle at Port-Patrick."

It was in vain for Archie to think of resistance, he was unarmed and helpless. Two of the soldiers laid hands on him and hurried him along until they reached the lower chambers of the castle. The governor unlocked a door, and with one of the torchbearers led the way down some narrow steps. These were some fifty in number, and then a level passage ran along for some distance. Another door was opened, and the fresh breeze blew upon them as they issued forth. They stood on some rocks at the foot of the promontory on which the castle stood. A large boat lay close at hand, drawn to the shore. Archie and the six soldiers entered her; four of the latter took the oars, and the others seated themselves by their prisoner, and then the boat rowed away, while the governor returned to aid in the defense of the castle.

The boat was but a quarter of a mile away when on the night air came the sound of a wild outburst of triumphant shouts which told that the Scots had won their way into the castle. With muttered curses the men bent to their oars and every minute took them further away from Knockbawn.

Archie was bitterly disappointed. He had reckoned confidently on the efforts of Douglas to deliver

him, and the possibility of his being sent off by sea
had not entered his mind. It seemed to him now
that his fate was sealed. He had noticed on
embarking that there were no other boats lying at
the foot of the promontory, and pursuit would
therefore be impossible.

After rowing eight hours the party reached Port-
Patrick, where Archie was delivered by the soldiers
to the governor with a message from their commander saying that the prisoner, Sir Archibald
Forbes, was a captive of great importance, and was,
by the orders of Sir Ingram de Umfraville, who had
captured him, to be sent on to Carlisle to the king
when a ship should be going thither. A fortnight
passed before a vessel sailed. Archie was placed in
irons and so securely guarded in his dungeon that
escape was altogether impossible. So harsh was
his confinement that he longed for the time when a
vessel would sail for Carlisle, even though he was
sure that the same fate which had attended so many
of Scotland's best and bravest knights awaited him
there.

The winds were contrary, and the vessel was ten
days upon the voyage. Upon reaching Carlisle
Archie was handed to the governor of the castle,
and the next morning was conducted to the presence of the king himself. The aged monarch, in
the last extremity of sickness, lay upon a couch.
Several of his nobles stood around him.

"So," he said as the prisoner was brought before
him, "this is Archibald Forbes, the one companion

of the traitor Wallace who has hitherto escaped my vengeance. So, young sir, you have ventured to brave my anger and to think yourself capable of coping with the Lion of England."

" I have done my utmost, sir king," Archie said firmly, " such as it was, for the freedom of my country. No traitor am I, nor was my leader Wallace. Nor he, nor I, ever took vow of allegiance to you, maintaining ever that the kings of England had neither claim nor right over Scotland. He has been murdered, foully and dishonorably, as you will doubtless murder me, and as you have killed many nobler knights and gentlemen; but others will take our places, and so the fight will go on until Scotland is free."

" Scotland will never be free," the king said with angry vehemence. " Rather than that, she shall cease to exist, and I will slay till there is not one of Scottish blood, man, woman, or child, to bear the name. Let him be taken to Berwick," he said; " there let him be exposed for a week in a cage outside the castle, that the people may see what sort of a man this is who matches himself against the might of England. Then let him be hung, drawn, and quartered, his head sent to London, and his limbs distributed between four Scotch cities."

" I go, sir king," Archie said, as the attendants advanced to seize him, " and at the end of the week I will meet you before the throne of God, for you, methinks, will have gone thither before me, and there will I tax you with all your crimes, with the slaughter of tens of thousands of Scottish men, women, and children, with cities destroyed and countries wasted, and with the murder in cold blood of a score of noble knights whose sole offense was that they fought for their native country."

With these words Archie turned and walked proudly from the king's presence. An involuntary murmur of admiration at his fearless bearing escaped from the knights and nobles assembled round the couch of the dying monarch.

When, two days later, Archie entered the gates of Berwick Castle the bells of the city were tolling, for a horseman had just ridden in with the news that Edward had expired on the evening before, being the 6th day of July, 1307, just at the moment when he was on the point of starting with the great army he had assembled to crush out the insurrection in Scotland.

So deep was his hate for the people who had dared to oppose his will that when dying he called before him his eldest son, and in the presence of his barons caused him to swear upon the saints that so soon as he should be dead his body should be boiled in a cauldron until the flesh should be separated from the bones, after which the flesh should be committed to the earth, but the bones preserved, and that, as often as the people of Scotland rebelled the military array of the kingdom should be summoned and the bones carried at the head of the army into Scotland. His heart he directed should be conveyed to and deposited in the Holy Land.

So died Edward I., a champion of the Holy Sepulcher, King of England, Lord of Ireland, Duke of Aquitaine, conqueror of Wales, and would-be conqueror of Scotland. In many respects his reign was a great and glorious one, for he was more than a great conqueror, he was, to England, a wise and noble king; and taken altogether he was perhaps the greatest of the Plantagenets.

Historians have striven to excuse and palliate his conduct toward Scotland. They have glossed over his crimes and tried to explain away the records of his deeds of savage atrocity, and to show that his claims to that kingdom, which had not a shadow of foundation save from the submission of her Anglo-Norman nobles, almost all of whom were his own vassals and owned estates in England, were just and righteous. Such is not the true function of history. Edward's sole claim to Scotland was that he was determined to unite under his rule England, Scotland, Wales, and Ireland, and he failed because the people of Scotland, deserted as they were by all their natural leaders, preferred death to such a slavery as that under which Ireland and Wales helplessly groaned. His dying wishes were not observed. His body was laid in Westminster Abbey, and on the tomb was inscribed, " Edward I. the mallet of the Scots."

CHAPTER XXIII.

THE ESCAPE FROM BERWICK.

ON entering the castle Archie was at once conducted to a sort of cage which had been constructed for a previous prisoner. On the outside of a small cell a framework of stout beams had been erected. It was seven feet in height, six feet wide, and three feet deep. The bars were four inches round, and six inches apart. There was a door leading into the cell behind. This was closed in the daytime, so that the prisoner remained in the cage in sight of passers-by, but at night the governor, who was a humane man, allowed the door to remain unlocked, so that the prisoner could enter the inner cell and lie down there.

The position of the cage was about twenty-five feet above the moat. The moat itself was some forty feet wide, and a public path ran along the other side, and people passing here had a full view of the prisoner. There were still many of Scottish birth in the town in spite of the efforts which Edward had made to convert it into a complete English colony, and although the English were in the majority, Archie was subject to but little insult or annoyance. Although for the present in English possession, Berwick had always been a Scotch town, and might yet again from the fortune of war fall into Scottish hands. Therefore even those most hostile to them felt that it would be prudent to restrain from any demonstrations against the Scottish prisoners, since in the event of the city again changing hands a bloody retaliation might be dealt them. Occasionally a passing boy would shout out an epithet of contempt or hatred or throw a stone at the prisoner, but such trifles were un- heeded by him. More often men or women passing would stop and gaze up at him with pitying looks, and would go away wiping their eyes.

Archie, after the first careful examination of his cell, at once abandoned any idea of escape from it. The massive bars would have defied the strength of twenty men, and he had no instrument of any sort with which he could cut them. There was, he felt, nothing before him but death; and although he feared this little for himself, he felt sad indeed as he thought of the grief of Marjory and his mother.

The days passed slowly. Five had gone without an incident, and but two remained, for he knew that there was no chance of any change in the sentence which Edward had passed, even were his son more disposed than he toward merciful measures to the Scots, which Archie had no warrant for supposing. The new king's time would be too closely engaged in the affairs entailed by his accession to rank, the arrangement of his father's funeral, and the details of the army advancing against Scotland, to give a thought to the prisoner whose fate had been determined by his father.

Absorbed in his own thoughts Archie seldom looked across the moat, and paid no heed to those who passed or who paused to look at him.

On the afternoon of the fifth day, however, his eye was caught by two women who were gazing up at the cage. It was the immobility of their attitude and the length of time which they continued to gaze at him, which attracted his attention.

In a moment he started violently and almost gave a cry, for in one of them he recognized his wife, Marjory. The instant that the women saw that he had observed them they turned away and walked carelessly and slowly along the road. Archie could hardly believe that his eyesight had not deceived him. It seemed impossible that Marjory, whom he deemed a hundred miles away, in his castle at Aberfilly, should be here in the town of Berwick, and yet when he thought it over he saw that it might well be so. There was indeed ample time for her to have made the journey two or three times while he had been lying in prison at Port-Patrick awaiting a ship. She would be sure, when the news reached her of his capture, that he would be taken to Edward at Carlisle, and that he would be either executed there or at Berwick. It was then by no means impossible, strange and wondrous as it appeared to him, that Marjory should be in Berwick.

Archie a prisoner in the cage at Berwick.—Page 386.

—*In Freedom's Cause.*

She was attired in the garment of a peasant woman of the better class, such as the wife of a small crofter or farmer, and remembering how she had saved his life before at Dunstaffnage, Archie felt that she had come hither to try to rescue him.

Archie's heart beat with delight and his eyes filled with tears at the devotion and courage of Marjory, and for the first time since he had been hurried into the boat on the night of his capture a feeling of hope entered his breast. Momentary as the glance had been which he had obtained of the face of Marjory's companion, Archie had perceived that it was in some way familiar to him. In vain he recalled the features of the various servants at Aberfilly, and those of the wives and daughters of the retainers of the estate; he could not recognize the face of the woman accompanying Marjory as belonging to any of them. His wife might, indeed, have brought with her some one from the estates at Ayr whom she had known from a child, but in that case Archie could not account for his knowledge of her. This, however, did not occupy his mind many minutes; it was assuredly one whom Marjory trusted, and that was sufficient for him. Then his thoughts turned wholly to his wife.

Any one who had noticed the prisoner's demeanor for the last few days would have been struck with the change which had come over it. Hitherto he had stood often for hours leaning motionless, with his arms crossed, in the corner of his cage, with head bent down and listless air, his thoughts only being busy; now he paced restlessly up and down his narrow limits, two steps each way and then a turn, like a caged beast; his hands were clenched, his breast heaved, his breath came fast, his head was thrown back, often he brushed his hand across his eyes, and rapid words came from his lips.

The sun sank. An hour later a jailer brought his jug of water and piece of bread, and then, without a word, retired, leaving as usual, the door into the cell open, but carefully locking and barring the inner door. Archie had a longer walk now, from the front of the cage to the back of the cell, and for three hours he paced up and down. Sometimes he paused and listened attentively. The sounds in the town gradually died away and all became still, save that he could hear the calls of the warder on the ʼattlement above him. The night was a very dark one and he could scarcely make out the gleam of water in the moat below.

Suddenly something struck him a sharp blow on the face and fell at his feet. He stooped and picked it up, it was an arrow with a wad of wool fastened round its point to prevent it from making a noise should it strike the wall or cage; to the other end was attached a piece of string. Archie drew it in until he felt that it was held firmly, then after a moment the hold relaxed somewhat, and the string again yielded as he drew it. It was now, he felt, taut from the other side of the moat. Presently a stout rope, amply sufficient to bear his weight, came into his hands. At the point of junction was attached some object done up in flannel. This he opened, and found that it was a fine saw and a small bottle containing oil. He fastened the rope securely to one of the bars and at once commenced to saw asunder one of the others. In five minutes two cuts had been noiselessly made, and a portion of the bar five feet long came away. He now tried the rope and found that it was tightly stretched, and evidently fixed to some object on the other side of the moat. He grasped it firmly with his arms and legs and slid rapidly down it.

In another minute he was grasped by some strong arms which checked his rapid progress and enabled him to gain his feet without the slightest noise. As he did so a woman threw her arms round him, and he exchanged a passionate but silent embrace with Marjory. Then she took his hand and with noise-less steps they proceeded down the road. He had, before starting, removed his shoes and put them in his pockets. Marjory and her companion had also removed their shoes, and even the keenest ears upon the battlements would have heard no sound as they proceeded along the road. Fifty yards further and they were among the houses. Here they stopped a minute and put on their shoes, and then continued their way. Not a word was spoken until they had traversed several streets and stopped at the door of a house in a quiet lane; it yielded to Marjory's touch, she and Archie entered, and their follower closed and fastened it after them.

The moment this was done Marjory threw her

arms round Archie's neck with a burst of tears of joy and relief. While Archie was soothing her the third person stirred up the embers on the hearth and threw on a handful of dry wood.

"And who is your companion?" Archie asked, after the first transports of joy and thankfulness were past.

"What! don't you recognize Cluny?" Marjory asked, laughing through her tears.

"Cluny! of course," Archie exclaimed, grasping his follower's hand in his. "I only caught a glimpse of your face and knew that it was familiar to me, but in vain tried to recall its owner. Why, Cluny, it is a long time since you went dressed as a girl into Ayr? And so it is my good friend who has shared my wife's dangers."

"He has done more than that, Archie," Marjory said, "for it was to him that I owe my first idea of coming here. The moment after the castle was taken and it was found that you had been carried off in a boat by the English, Cluny started to tell me the news. Your mother and I were beside ourselves with grief, and Cluny, to comfort us, said, 'Do not despair yet, my lady; my lord shall not be killed by the English if I can prevent it. The master and I have been in a good many dangers, and have always come out of them safe; it shall not be my fault if he does not slip through their hands yet.' 'Why, what can you do, Cluny?' I said. 'I don't know what I can do yet,' he replied; 'that must depend upon circumstances. My lord is sure to be taken to Carlisle, and I shall go south to see if I cannot get him out of prison. I have often gone among the English garrisons disguised as a woman, and no one in Carlisle is likely to ask me my business there.' It was plain to me at once that if Cluny could go to your aid, so could I, and I at once told him that I should accompany him. Cluny raised all sorts of objections, but to these I would not listen, but brought him to my will by saying, that if he thought my being with him would add to his difficulties I would go alone, but that go I certainly would. So without more ado we got these dresses and made south. We had a few narrow escapes of falling into the hands of parties of English, but at last we crossed the frontier and made to Carlisle. Three days later we heard of your arrival, and the next morning all men were talking about your defiance of the king, and that you had been sent to Berwick for execution at the end of the week. So we journeyed hither and got here the day after you arrived. The first step was to find a Scotchwoman whom we might trust. This, by great luck, we did, and Mary Martin, who lives in this house, is a true Scotchwoman, and will help us to the extent of her power; she is poor, for her husband, who is an Englishman, had for some time been ill, and died but yesterday. He was, by what she says, a hard man and a cruel, and his death is no grief to her, and Mary will, if she can, return with her daughter to Roxburgh, where her relations live, and where she married her husband, who was a soldier in the English garrison there."

"But, Marjory," Archie said, "have you thought how we are to escape hence; though I am free from the castle I am still within the walls of Berwick, and when, to-morrow, they find that I have escaped, they will search every nook and corner of the town. I had best without delay try and make my way over the walls."

"That was the plan Cluny and I first thought of," Marjory replied; "but owing to the raids of the Douglas on the border, so strict a watch is kept on the walls that it would be difficult indeed to pass. Cluny has tried a dozen times each night, but the watch is so vigilant that he has each time failed to make his way past them, but has been challenged and has had several arrows discharged at him. The guard at the gates is extremely strict, and all carts that pass in and out are searched. Could you have tried to pass before your escape was known you might no doubt have done so in disguise, but the alarm will be given before the gates are open in the morning, and your chance of passing through undetected then would be small indeed. The death of the man Martin suggested a plan to me. I have proposed it to his wife, and she has fallen in with it. I have promised her a pension for her life should we succeed, but I believe she would have done it even without reward, for she is a true Scotchwoman. When she heard who it was that I was trying to rescue, she said at once she would risk anything to save the life of one of Scotland's best and bravest champions; while, on the other hand, she cares not enough for her husband to offer any objection to my plans for the disposal of his body."

" But, what are your plans, Marjory ?"

" All the neighbors know that Martin is dead; they believe that Cluny is Mary's sister and I her niece, and she has told them that she shall return with us to Roxburgh. Martin was a native of a village four miles hence, and she is going to bury him with his fathers there. Now I have proposed to her that Martin shall be buried beneath the wood store here, and that you shall take his place in the coffin."

" It is a capital idea, Marjory," Archie said, " and will assuredly succeed if any plan can do so. The only fear is that the search will be so hot in the morning that the soldiers may even insist upon looking into the coffin."

" We have thought of that," Marjory said, "and dare not risk it. We must expect every house to be searched in the morning, and have removed some tiles in the attic. At daybreak you must creep out on the roof, replace the tiles, and remain hidden there until the search is over. Martin will be laid in the coffin. Thus, even should they lift the lid, no harm will come of it. Directly they have gone, Cluny will bring you down, and you and he dig the grave in the floor of the woodshed and place Martin there, then you will take his place in the coffin, which will be placed in a cart already hired, and Cluny, I, Mrs. Martin, and her daughter, will then set out with it."

Soon after daybreak the quick strokes of the alarm-bell at the castle told the inhabitants of Berwick that a prisoner had escaped. Archie at once betook himself to his place of concealment on the roof. He replaced the tiles, and Cluny carefully obliterated all signs of the place of exit from within. A great hubbub had by this time arisen in the street. Trumpets were blowing and parties of soldiers moving about in all directions. The gates remained unopened, orders being given that none should pass through without a special order from the governor.

The sentries on the wall were doubled, and then a house-to-house search was commenced, every possible place of concealment being rummaged from basement to attic. Presently the searchers entered the lane in which Mrs. Martin lived. The latch was ere long lifted, and a sergeant and six soldiers burst into the room. The sight which they beheld quieted their first noisy exclamations. Four women in deep mourning were kneeling by a rough coffin placed on trestles. One of them gave a faint scream as they entered, and Mary Martin, rising to her feet, said:

"What means this rough intrusion?"

"It means," the sergeant said, "that a prisoner has escaped from the castle, one Archibald Forbes, a pestilent Scotch traitor. He has been aided by friends from without, and as the sentries were watchful all night, he must be hidden somewhere in the town, and every house is to be searched."

"You can search if you will," the woman said, resuming the position on her knees. "As you see, this is a house of mourning, seeing that my husband is dead, and is to-day to be buried in his native village, three miles away."

"He won't be buried to-day," the sergeant said; "for the gates are not to be opened save by a special order from the governor. Now, lads," he went on, turning to the men, "search the place from top to bottom, examine all the cupboards and sound the floors, turn over all the wood in the shed, and leave not a single place unsearched where a mouse could be hid."

The soldiers scattered through the house, and were soon heard knocking the scanty furniture about and sounding the floors and walls. At last they returned saying that nothing was to be found.

"And now," the sergeant said, "I must have a look in that coffin. Who knows but what the traitor Scot may be hid in there!"

Mrs. Martin leaped to her feet.

"You shall not touch the coffin," she said; "I will not have the remains of my husband disturbed." The sergeant pushed her roughly aside, and with the end of his pike pried up the lid of the coffin, while Mrs. Martin and the other three mourners screamed lustily and wrung their hands in the greatest grief at this desecration of the dead.

Just as the sergeant opened the coffin and satisfied himself that a dead man really lay within, an officer, attracted by the screams, entered the room.

"What is this, sergeant?" he asked angrily. "The orders were to search the house, but none were given you to trouble the inmates."

Mrs. Martin began volubly to complain of the conduct of the soldiers in wrenching open the coffin.

"It was a necessary duty, my good woman," the officer said, "seeing that a living man might have been carried away instead of a dead one; however, I see all is right."

"Oh, kind sir!" Mrs. Martin said, sobbing, "is it true what this man tells me, that there is no passage through the gates to-day? I have hired a cart to take away my husband's body; the grave is dug, and the priest will be waiting. Kind sir, I pray of you to get me a pass to sally out with it, together with my daughter, sister and niece."

"Very well," the officer said kindly, "I will do as you wish. I shall be seeing the governor presently to make my report to him; and as I have myself seen the dead body can vouch that no ruse is intended. But assuredly no pass will be given for any man to accompany you; and the Scot, who is a head and shoulders taller than any of you, would scarcely slip out in a woman's garment. When will the cart be here?"

"At noon," the woman replied.

"Very well; an hour before that time a soldier will bring you the pass. Now, sergeant, have you searched the rest of the house?"

"Yes, sir; thoroughly, and nothing suspicious has been found."

"Draw off your men, then, and proceed with your search elsewhere."

No sooner had the officer and men departed than Cluny ran upstairs, and removing two of the tiles, whispered to Archie that all was clear. The hole was soon enlarged, and Archie re-entering, the pair descended to the woodshed which adjoined the kitchen, and there, with a spade and mattock which Cluny had purchased on the preceding day, they set to work to dig a grave. In two hours it was completed. The body of John Martin was lowered into it, the earth replaced and trodden down hard, and the wood again piled on to it.

At eleven o'clock a soldier entered with the governor's pass ordering the soldier at the gate to allow a cart with the body of John Martin, accompanied by four women, to pass out from the town.

At the appointed time the cart arrived. Archie now took his place in the coffin. His face was whitened, and a winding-sheet wrapped round him, lest by an evil chance any should insist on again looking into the coffin. Then some neighbors came in and assisted in placing the coffin in the cart. The driver took his place beside it, and the four women, with their hoods drawn over their heads, fell in behind it weeping bitterly.

When they arrived at the gate the officer in charge carefully read the order, and then gave the order for the gate to be opened. "But stop," he said, "this pass says nothing about a driver, and though this man in no way resembles the description of the

doughty Scot, yet as he is not named in the pass I
cannot let him pass." There was a moment's pause
of consternation, and then Cluny said:

"Sister Mary, I will lead the horse. When all is
in readiness, and the priest waits, we cannot turn
back on such a slight cause." As the driver of the
cart knew Mary Martin, he offered no objection,
and descended from his seat. Cluny took the reins,
and, walking by the side of the horse's head, led him
through the gates as these were opened, the others
following behind. As soon as they were through,
the gates closed behind them, and they were safely
out of the town of Berwick.

So long as they were within sight of the walls
they proceeded at a slow pace without change of
position, and although Cluny then quickened the
steps of the horse, no other change was made until
two miles further they reached a wood. Then
Cluny leaped into the cart and wrenched off the lid
of the coffin. It had been but lightly nailed down,
and being but roughly made there were plenty of
crevices through which the air could pass.

"Quick, Sir Archie!" he said, "let us get this
thing out of the cart before any person happens to
come along."

The coffin was lifted from the cart, and carried
some short distance into the wood. A few vigorous
kicks separated the planks which composed it.
These were taken and thrust separately among
bushes at some little distance from each other.
Cluny then unrolled the bundle which he had brought

from the cart, and handed to Archie a suit of clothes fitted for a farmer. These Archie quickly put on, then he returned to the cart, which he mounted, and took the reins. The others got up behind him and seated themselves on the straw in the bottom of the cart. Then Archie gave the horse a smart cut with his whip, and the cart proceeded at a steady trot along the road to the west.

CHAPTER XXIV.

THE PROGRESS OF THE WAR.

A MILE or two after leaving Berwick the cart had left the main road running by the coast through Dunbar to Edinburgh, and had struck west by a country track. But few houses were met with, as the whole of the country within many miles of the sea had been harried and devastated by the various English armies which had advanced from Berwick. After proceeding for some miles they came to a point where the track they had been following terminated at a little hamlet among the hills. Here they left the cart, making an arrangement with one of the villagers to drive it back on the morrow into Berwick. They were now beyond all risk of pursuit, and need fear nothing further until they reached the great north roads running from Carlisle to Edinburgh and Stirling. Cluny therefore resumed male attire. They had no difficulty in purchasing a couple of swords from the peasants of the village, and armed with these they started with Marjory and the two women over the hills. It was early autumn now; the weather was magnificent, and they made the distance in quiet stages, and crossing the Pentlands came down upon Aberfilly without meeting with a single danger or obstacle.

It needs not to describe the joy of Archie's mother at his return. The news spread like lightning among the tenantry, and in an hour after the wayfarers reached the castle men and women could be seen flocking over the hills at the top of their speed to express their delight and enthusiasm at their lord's return. By nightfall every tenant on the estate, save those prevented by age or illness, had assembled at the castle, and the rejoicings which had taken place at the marriage of their lord were but tame and quiet beside the boisterous enthusiasm which was now exhibited.

Although Marjory had at first been welcomed for the sake of her husband, the fact that she was a Kerr had excited a deep though hidden hostility to her in the minds both of those who had been her father's vassals at Aberfilly, and the old retainers of the Forbeses at Glen Cairn. The devotion and courage which she had shown in the defense of the castle and in the enterprise for the rescue of their lord swept away every vestige of this feeling, and henceforth Marjory ranked in their affections with Archie himself, and there was not a man upon the estate but felt that he could die for her if needs be.

After a week's stay at home Archie rode away and joined the king, taking, however, but four or five retainers with him. Bruce received him with extreme warmth. He had heard of his capture, and the news that he was condemned to die at Berwick

had also reached him, and he had no doubt but
Archie had shared the fate which had befallen his
own brothers and so many of his bravest friends.
His pleasure, therefore, equaled his surprise when
his brave follower rode into his camp. Many of
Archie's friends assembled as soon as it was known
that he had arrived; and after the first greetings
the king asked him for a recital of the means by
which he had escaped from the fate decreed him by
Edward. Archie related the whole story, and at its
conclusion the king called to his attendants to bring
goblets and wine.

"Sirs," he said, "let us drink to the health of
Mistress Marjory Forbes, one of the bravest and
truest of Scotch women. Would to heaven that
all the men of our country were animated by as
noble and courageous feelings! Our friend, Sir
Archibald Forbes, has indeed won a jewel, and I
take no small credit to myself that I was the first
who advised him to make Mistress Kerr his wife."

The toast was given with enthusiasm; but Archie
afterward protested against the king assuming any
credit to himself in the matter, since, although it
was true that he had advised him to marry Mistress
Mary Kerr, he had wished him to abandon, for her
sake, Mistress Marjory, the niece of Alexander
MacDougall, who had set him free from her uncle's
hold of Dunstaffnage.

"Now, Archie," the king said, when they were
again alone together, "I suppose, seeing that you
have come hither without your following, that you

wish for a time to remain quiet at home, and seeing
that you have suffered severe imprisonment and a
grievous risk of death in my cause, methinks you
have well earned the right to rest quiet for awhile
with your brave lady.　At present I can dispense
with the services of your retainers.　Most of the
low country is now in my hands, and the English
garrisons dare not venture out of their strong
places.　The army that the King of England
collected to crush us has been, I hear, much dis-
organized by his death, and the barons will doubtless
wring concessions and privileges from his son before
they spread their banners to the wind again.
From all reports the new king has but little of his
father's ability and energy, and months may elapse
before any serious effort is made against us.　I am
despatching my brother Edward to join Douglas in
subduing Galloway, and during his absence I shall
be content to remain here in the field with a small
following, for the English governors of the towns
will, methinks, stand only on the defensive, until a
strong army marches north from England.　When
Galloway is subdued the lowlands will be all in my
hands save for the English garrisons, and I shall on
Edward's return set myself to punish the Comyns
and the other traitor nobles of the north, who are
well-nigh all hand and glove with the English.　So
long as Scotland has such powerful enemies in her
midst she cannot hope to cope with the forces which
England can send against her.　Alone and united
the task is one which will tax her strength to the

utmost, seeing that England is in wealth and
population so far her superior, and Edward disposes
of the force of Ireland, of Wales, and of Gascony;
therefore my first task must be to root out these
traitor nobles from among us.   When I move north
I shall need your company and your strength; but
until Edward has cleared the English out of Galloway, captured the strongholds, and reduced it to
obedience, you can stop in Aberfilly, and there at
times, when I have no enterprise on hand and can
take a few days, I will come and rest if you will
give me hospitality."

So until the following spring Archie Forbes remained quietly and most happily at home.   Several
times the king came and stayed a few days at Aberfilly, where he was safe against surprise and
treachery.   Not long after Archie's return home
Father Anselm arrived, to Archie's satisfaction and
the great joy of Marjory, and took up his abode
there.

In the spring Archie, with his retainers, joined
the king, who was gathering his army for his march
into the north.   During the winter Galloway had
been subdued, and Douglas being left in the south
as commander there, Edward Bruce joined his
brother, around whom also gathered the Earl of
Lennox, Sir Gilbert de la Haye, and others.   The
position in Scotland was now singular: the whole
of the country south of the Forth was favorable to
Bruce, but the English held Roxburgh, Jedburgh,
Dumfries, Castle Douglas, Ayr, Bothwell, Edin-

burgh, Linlithgow, Stirling, and Dumbarton. North
of the Forth nearly the whole of the country was
hostile to the king, and the fortresses of Perth,
Dundee, Forfar, Brechin, Aberdeen, Inverness, and
many smaller holds, were occupied by English
garrisons.

The center of hostility to Bruce, north of the
Forth, lay in the two great earls, the Comyns of
Badenoch and Buchan, and their allies. Between
them and Bruce a hatred existed beyond that caused
by their taking opposite sides. Comyn of Badenoch
was the son of the man Bruce had slain at Dumfries, while Buchan hated him even more, since his
wife, the countess, had espoused the cause of Bruce
and had crowned him at Scone, and was now shame-
fully imprisoned in the cage at Berwick. It must
be supposed that Buchan's anger against his countess was as deep and implacable as that of Edward
himself, for, as the English king's most powerful
ally in Scotland, he could surely have obtained the
pardon and release of his wife had he desired it. On
the other hand, Bruce had a private grudge against
Comyn, for upon him had been conferred Bruce's
lordship of Annandale, and he had entered into
possession and even occupied the family castle of
Lochmaben.

The king and his army marched north, and were
joined by Alexander and Simon Fraser, with their
followers. They marched to Inverness, which,
with various other castles in the north, they captured. All of these castles were, when taken,

destroyed, as Bruce had determined to leave no strongholds in the land for the occupation of his enemies. He himself could not spare men to hold them, and their capture was useless if upon his retirement they could again be occupied by the enemy. Returning southward they were encountered by an army under Buchan, composed of his own retainers and a party of English. This force was completely defeated.

To the consternation of his followers Bruce was now attacked by a wasting illness, which so enfeebled him that he was unable to sit on his horse ; it was the result of the many privations and hardships which he had undergone since the fight at Methven. His brother, Lennox, the Frasers, and Archie Forbes held a council and agreed that rest for some time was absolutely necessary for the king, and that sea air might be beneficial to him. They therefore resolved to move eastward to the castle of Slaines, on the seacoast near Peterhead. That such a step was attended by great peril they well knew, for the Comyns would gather the whole strength of the Highlands, with accessions from the English garrisons, and besiege them there. The king's health, however, was a paramount consideration ; were he to die the blow might be fatal to Scotland, accordingly the little force marched eastward. They reached Slaines without interruption, and as they expected the castle was soon surrounded and besieged by the forces of Buchan, who had been joined by Sir John Mowbray and Sir David de

Brechin, nephew of the King of England. For some time the siege went on, but the assailants gained but little advantage, and indeed trusted rather to famine than force to reduce the castle.

Weeks passed on, and although his followers thought that he was somewhat better, the king's health improved but slowly. Provisions now began to run very short. When they had come nearly to an end the Scots determined to sally out and cut their way through the vastly superior strength of the enemy. The king was placed in a litter, his mounted knights and followers surrounded him, and round these the footmen formed a close clump of pikes; the hundred men from Aberfilly formed the front rank, as these could be best relied upon to withstand the charge of the English horse. The gates were thrown open, and in close ranks the garrison sallied out, forming, as soon as they passed through, in the order arranged. So close and serried was the hedge of spears, so quiet and determined the attitude of the men, that numerous as they were, the men of Buchan and the English lords shrank from an encounter with such adversaries, and with the banner of the king and his knights flying in their center the little band marched on through the lines of the besiegers without the latter striking a blow to hinder their way.

Without interruption the royalists proceeded to Strathbogie. The satisfaction of the king at the daring exploit by which he had been rescued from such imminent peril did more for him than medi-

cine or change of air, and to the joy of his followers
he began to recover his strength. He was then
moved down to the river Don. Here Buchan and
his English allies made a sudden attack upon his
quarters, killing some of the outposts. This attack
roused the spirit and energy of the king, and he
immediately called for his war-horse and armor and
ordered his men to prepare for action. His followers remonstrated with him, but he declared that
this attack by his enemies had cured him more
speedily than medicine could have done, and heading his troops he issued forth and came upon the
enemy near Old Meldrum, where, after a desperate
fight, Buchan and his confederates were defeated
with great slaughter on Christmas day, 1307.
Buchan and Mowbray fled into England. Brechin
took refuge in his own castle of Brechin, where
he was afterward besieged and forced to surrender.

Bruce now marched into the territory of Comyn,
where he took a terrible vengeance for the long
adhesion of his hated enemy to England. The
whole country was wasted with fire and sword, the
people well-nigh exterminated, and the very forests
destroyed. So terrible was the devastation that for
generations afterward men spoke of the harrying
of Buchan as a terrible and exceptional act of
vengeance.

The castle of Aberdeen was next invested. The
English made great efforts for its succor, but the
citizens joined Bruce, and a united attack being
made upon the castle it was taken by assault and

razed to the ground. The king and his forces then moved into Angus. Here the English strongholds were all taken, the castle of Forfar being assaulted and carried by a leader who was called Phillip, a forester of Platane. With the exception of Perth, the most important fortress north of the Forth, and a few minor holds, the whole of the north of Scotland was now in the king's hands. It the meantime Sir James Douglas, in the south, had again taken his paternal castle and had razed it to the ground. The forests of Selkirk and Jedburgh, with the numerous fortresses of the district, were brought under the king's authority, and the English were several times defeated. In the course of these adventures Sir James came across Alexander Stewart, Thomas Randolph, the king's nephew, who, after being taken prisoner at Methven, had joined the English party, and Adam O'Gordon. They advanced with a much superior force to capture him, but were signally defeated. O'Gordon escaped into England, but Stewart and Randolph were taken.

This was a fortunate capture, for Randolph afterward became one of the king's most valiant knights and the wisest of his counselors. After this action Douglas marched north and joined the king. The latter sternly reproached Randolph for having foresworn his allegiance and joined the English. Randolph answered hotly and was committed by his uncle to solitary confinement, where he presently came to a determination to renew his allegiance to Bruce, and henceforward fought faithfully and gallantly under him.

Galloway had risen again, and Edward Bruce, with Sir Archie Forbes, was detached to reduce it. It was a hard task, for the local chiefs were supported by Sir Ingram de Umfraville and Sir John de St. John; these knights, with twelve hundred followers, met the Scots on the banks of the Cree, which separates the counties of Kirkcudbright and Wigton, and although greatly superior in numbers, were completely defeated by the Scottish pikemen, and compelled to take refuge in the castle of Butele. Edward Bruce and Archie continued the task of subjugating the country; but St. John having retired to England, returned with fifteen hundred men-at-arms, and with this strong force set out in pursuit of the small body of Scots, of whom he thought to make an easy capture. Then occurred one of the most singular and brilliant feats of arms that took place in a war in which deeds of daring abounded. Edward Bruce having heard from the country people of the approach of his adversaries placed his infantry in a strong position, and then, with Archie Forbes and the fifty men-at-arms who constituted his cavalry, went out to reconnoiter the approach of the English. The morning was thick and misty. Ignorant of each other's position, the two forces were in close vicinity, when the fog suddenly lifted, and Edward Bruce and Archie beheld close to them the overwhelming force of St. John, within bowshot distance. It was too late to fly. Edward Bruce exclaimed to Archie:

"There is nothing for it but to charge them."

"Let us charge them," Archie replied.

The two leaders, setting spurs to their horses, and closely followed by their fifty retainers, dashed like a thunderbolt upon the mass of the English men-at-arms, before these, taken equally by surprise, had time to form, and burst clean through them, over-throwing and slaying many, and causing the great-est confusion and surprise. Riding but a short dis-tance on, the Scots turned, and again burst through the English lines. Numbers of the English were slain, and many others turned rein. A third time the Scots charged with equally fatal effect. The English were completely routed. Many were killed and many taken prisoners, and the rest rode for England at their best speed. History scarcely recalls another instance of fifty men routing in fair fight fifteen hundred. This extraordinary success was followed by a victory over Sir Roland of Galloway and Donald of the Isles on the banks of the Dee, the Lord of the Isles being made prisoner; and eventually the whole country was reduced to obedience, with the exception of one or two garri-sons, no less than thirteen castles being captured, in addition to the victories gained in the field.

Galloway being restored to order, Archie Forbes returned home, and remained for two or three months with his wife and mother. He was then summoned by the king to join him again, as he was about to march to reduce the region over which his deadly foes Alexander and John of Lorne held sway. The country into which the royal army

now penetrated was extremely mountainous and
difficult, but they made their way as far as the
head of Loch Awe, where Alexander and John of
Lorne, with two thousand men, were gathered to
dispute the passage. The position was an extremely strong one, and the Lornes were confident that
it could not be forced. Immediately to the north
of the head of the lake rises the steep and lofty
mountain Ben Cruachan. From the head of the
lake flows the river Awe connecting it with Loch
Etive, and the level space between the foot of the
mountain and the river is only wide enough for
two to ride abreast. This passage was known as
the Pass of Brander, and the Lornes might well believe that their position was unassailable.

Before advancing into the pass Bruce detached
Douglas, with Sir Alexander Fraser, Sir William
Wiseman, and Sir Andrew Grey, with a body of
lightly armed infantry and archers. These, un-
noticed by the enemy, climbed the side of the
mountain, and going far up it, passed along until
they got behind and above the enemy. The king
ordered his main body to lay aside all defensive
armor so that they could more easily climb the hill
and come to a hand-to-hand conflict with the enemy.
Then he moved along toward the narrow pass. As
they approached it the men of Lorne hurled down a
torrent of rocks from the hillside above.

With a few heavy-armed men Bruce pushed forward by the water side, while Archie Forbes led
the main body up the hillside. The climb was stiff

and difficult, and many were swept down by the rocks hurled by the enemy; but at last they came to close quarters with the foe, and a desperate struggle ensued.

In the meantime Douglas and his party had attacked the defenders from the other side, at first showering arrows among them, and then falling upon them with sword and battle-axe. Thus attacked in front and rear, the men of Lorne lost heart and gave way. On both sides the royalists pressed them hotly, and at last they broke from the hillside and fled down to the river, intending to cross by a wooden bridge and destroy it behind them, but before many had passed Douglas with his followers arrived upon the spot and seized the bridge, cutting off their retreat. Great numbers of the men of Lorne were slain, and the survivors made their escape up the mountain side again. The Lornes themselves were on board some galleys on Loch Awe, their intention having been to land in Bruce's rear when he was fairly entangled in the narrow pass. On witnessing the utter discomfiture of their followers they rowed rapidly away, and landed far down the lake. Alexander fled to England, where he ended his life.

Bruce now advanced through the country of Lorne, which, having never suffered from the English raids that had over and over again devastated the rest of Scotland, was rich and flourishing, and large quantities of booty were obtained. Dunstaffnage was besieged and captured, and having received hostages from all the minor chiefs for their good behavior the king and his army returned to Glasgow.

In the following spring a truce was negotiated by the intervention of the King of France between the belligerents; but its duration was but short, for so long as English nobles held estates and occupied castles in Scotland breaches of the peace would be constantly occurring. Bruce besieged the castle of Rutherglen, near Glasgow; but Edward despatched the Earl of Gloucester to raise the siege, and as Bruce's army was still small he was forced to retire at his approach.

In February, 1309, the clergy of Scotland assembled in a provincial council at Dundee, and issued a declaration in favor of Bruce as lawful king of Scotland. In this document they set forth that although Baliol was made king of Scotland by the King of England, Bruce, the grandfather of the king, was always recognized by the people as being nearest in right; and they said: "If any one, on the contrary, claim right to the aforesaid kingdom in virtue of letters in time past sealed, and containing the consent of the people and the commons, know ye that all this took place in fact by force and violence which could not at the time be resisted, and through multiplied fears, bodily tortures, and various terrors."

This document was sealed by all the bishops, as representing the clergy. A similar document was drawn up and signed by the estates of Scotland.

Therefore, henceforth Bruce could claim to be the king not only as crowned and by right, but by the approval and consent of the clergy and people of Scotland. A few months afterward James, the Steward of Scotland, whose course had ever been vacillating, died, and his son, Walter, a loyal Scotsman, succeeded him. He afterward married the king's daughter, Marjory, and became the founder of the royal line of Stuart.

CHAPTER XXV.

THE CAPTURE OF A STRONGHOLD.

WHILE Bruce had by his energy and courage been wresting Scotland, step by step, from the English, no serious effort had been made by the latter to check his progress. Small bodies of troops had from time to time been sent from the north; but the king had made no great efforts, like those of his father, to reduce the country to obedience by the exercise of the whole strength of England. Edward II. differed widely from his father in disposition. At times he was roused to fits of spasmodic energy, but for the most part he was sunk in sloth and supineness. He angered and irritated his barons by his fondness for unworthy favorites, and was engaged in constant broils with them.

So-called governors of Scotland were frequently appointed and as often superseded, but no effectual aid was given them to enable them to check the ever-spreading insurrection. But Perth was now threatened by Bruce; and the danger of this, the strongest and most important northern fortress, roused Edward from his lethargy. A fleet was fitted out for the Tay. Troops, under the Earl of

Ulster, were engaged to be transported by an English fleet of forty ships, supplied by the seaports, and intended to co-operate with John of Lorne in the west. Edward himself, with a powerful army, accompanied by the Lords Gloucester, Warrenne, Percy, Clifford, and others, advanced into Scotland as far as Renfrew. Bruce could oppose no effectual resistance in the field to so large a force, but he used the tactics which Wallace had adopted with such success. The country through which the English were advancing was wasted. Flocks and herds were driven off, and all stores of grain burned and destroyed. His adherents, each with their own retainers, hung upon the skirts of the English army, cutting off small parties, driving back bodies going out in search of provisions or forage, making sudden night attacks, and keeping the English in a state of constant watchfulness and alarm, but always retiring on the approach of any strong force, and avoiding every effort of the English to bring on an engagement.

The invaders were soon pressed by want of provisions, and horses died from lack of forage. The great army was therefore obliged to fall back to Berwick without having struck a single effective blow. After this Edward remained inactive at Berwick for eight months, save that he once again crossed the border and advanced as far as Roxburgh, but only to retreat without having accomplished anything. The Earls of Gloucester and Warrenne reduced the forest of Selkirk and the district, and restored the

English power there; while the king's favorite, Piers Gaveston, Earl of Cornwall, went by sea to Perth and tried to reduce the surrounding country, but the Scotch, as usual, retired before him, and he, too, after a time, returned to Berwick. The efforts of the defenders to starve out the invading armies of England were greatly aided by the fact that at this time a great famine raged both in England and Scotland, and the people of both countries were reduced to a condition of want and suffering. Not only did the harvest fail, but disease swept away vast numbers of cattle and sheep, and in many places the people were forced to subsist upon the flesh of horses, dogs, and other animals.

During the years which had elapsed since the battle of Methven, Bruce had never been enabled to collect a force in any way worthy of the name of an army. His enterprises had been a succession of daring feats performed by small bodies of men. Even now, when the nobles dared no longer openly oppose him, they remained sullenly aloof, and the captures of the English strongholds were performed either by the king or his brother Edward, with their retainers from Annandale and Carrick; by Douglas with the men of Douglasdale; or by some simple knights like Archie Forbes, the Frasers, Boyle and a few others, each leading their own retainers in the field. The great mass of the people still held aloof, and neither town nor country sent their contingents to his aid. This was not to be wondered at, so fearfully had all suffered from the wholesale vengeance of Edward after the battle of Falkirk.

Great successes had certainly attended Bruce, but these had been rendered possible only by the absence of any great effort on the part of England, and all believed that sooner or later Edward would arouse himself, and with the whole strength of England, Ireland, and Wales again crush out the movement, and carry fire and sword through Scotland. Still the national spirit was rising.

Archie Forbes divided his time pretty equally between the field and home, never taking with him, when he joined the king, more than a third of the entire strength of his retainers; thus all had time to attend to their farms and the wants of their families, and cheerfully yielded obedience to the call to arms when the time came.

One day while the king was stopping for a few days' rest at Aberfilly, a horseman rode in.

"I have great news, sire," he said. "Linlithgow has been captured from the English."

"That were good news, indeed," the king said; "but it can scarce be possible, seeing that we have no men-at-arms in the neighborhood."

"It has been done by no men-at-arms, my liege," the messenger said; "but as Forfar was taken by Phillip the Forester and his mates, so has Linlithgow been captured by a farmer and his comrades, one William Bunnock."

It was indeed true. The castle of Linlithgow, forming as it did a link between the two strongholds of Edinburgh and Stirling, was a place of great importance and was strongly garrisoned by the English. Naturally the whole country round suffered severely from the oppressions of the garrison, who supplied themselves by force with such provisions and stores as were needful for them. Payment was of course made to some extent, as the country otherwise would speedily have been deserted and the land left untilled ; but there was almost necessarily much oppression and high-handedness. Bunnock, hearing of the numerous castles which had been captured by the king and his friends with mere handfuls of followers, determined at last upon an attempt to expel the garrison of Linlithgow. He went about among his friends and neighbors, and found many ready to join his enterprise. These one night placed themselves in ambush among some bushes hard by the castle gate. Bunnock himself concealed eight chosen men with arms in a wagon of hay. The horses were driven by a stout peasant with a short hatchet under his belt, while Bunnock walked carelessly beside the wagon. As he was in the habit of supplying the garrison with corn and forage, the gate was readily opened on his approach. As soon as the wagon was exactly between the gateposts Bunnock gave the signal and struck down the warder at the gate ; the driver with his hatchet cut the traces, the men leaped up from their concealment in the hay, and the main body lying in ambush close by rushed up, and, taken wholly by surprise, unarmed and unprepared, the garrison was speedily overpowered and the castle taken.

It was in the spring of 1311 that this important capture took place. Bruce, as usual, had the castle leveled to the ground. Bunnock was rewarded by a grant of land which still bears his name, softened into Binney. Again the English made preparations for a renewed invasion, but the barons were too much occupied by their private broils and their quarrels with the king to assemble at his order, and nothing came of it. Bruce's position at home was so established that he resolved upon a counter invasion, and accordingly, having assembled a larger force than had hitherto gathered under his banner, crossed the border near the Solway, burned and plundered the district round Gilsland, ravaged Tynedale, and after eight days' havoc returned with much booty into Scotland. In the following month he again entered England, carried fire and sword through the country as far as Corbridge, swept Tynedale, ravaged Durham, and after levying contributions for fifteen days returned with much booty to Scotland.

Although the English made much outcry at this invasion, the English author of the Chronicle of Lanercost, whose monastery was occupied by the king during the raid, distinctly states that he slew none save in actual conflict; and again, that though "all the goods of the country were carried away, they did not burn houses or slay men." Thus, though Bruce's wife and daughter were still prisoners in England, though his brothers had been executed in cold blood, he conducted his warfare in

England in a manner which contrasts strongly indeed with the conduct of the English in Scotland.

After this Bruce marched north again and laid siege to Perth. For six weeks he invested the town, but without making any impression. Then he retired his forces as if abandoning the attempt. At night, however, he returned, ladders were placed in the ditches against the walls, and with his knights he led his followers on to the assault. The garrison were carousing in honor of their successful defense and the defeat of the enemy, and taken wholly by surprise were unable to oppose a vigorous resistance, and all were killed or captured. Some accounts say that the English soldiers were made prisoners, and the renegade Scots fighting with them were put to the sword; while others affirm that all who were taken prisoners were spared.

Another incursion into England followed the fall of Perth. Hexham, Corbridge, and Durham were destroyed. Douglas penetrated as far as Hartlepool and an immense spoil was carried off, until the people of the bishopric purchased a truce for the sum of two thousand pounds and those of Northumberland, Cumberland, and Westmoreland bought off the invaders at a like price.

Carlisle was assaulted by Douglas, but unsuccessfully. He also attempted to surprise Berwick by a night attack, and had placed his scaling-ladders against the wall, when the garrison was alarmed by the barking of a dog, and the assailants were re-

pulsed. The Scots recrossed the frontier laden with
an enormous booty.

The king himself now entered Galloway and reduced the four remaining strongholds held by the
English there—the castles of Butel, Dalswinton,
Lochmaben, and Tibbers. He then proceeded to
Dumfries, which he forced to surrender, and entered
it as the victorious King of Scotland, just seven
years after the time when he had commenced the
war by expelling the English justiciaries.

Archie Forbes did not accompany the king in this
campaign. He had indeed been summoned, but
just before the army started on its raid into England
Bruce was lamenting, in Archie's hearing, that the
continued possession of the strong castle of Dunottar on the east coast still afforded the English an
opportunity for creating diversions in the north, by
landing troops there.

"If you will permit me, sire," Archie said, "I
will undertake its capture with my retainers. It is
doubtless too strong to be captured by open assault
with such a strength, but as Douglas has thrice
taken Castle Douglas by stratagem, 'tis hard if I
cannot find some way for capturing Dunottar."

"Be it so, Sir Archie," the king said. "If you
succeed you will have done good service indeed ;
and as I know that though ever ready to buckle on
your armor when I need you, you would yet rather
live quiet at Aberfilly with your fair wife, I promise
you that if you capture Dunottar, for a year and a
day you and your retainers shall have rest, except

if the English cross the border in such force that the arm of every Scotchman able to wield a sword is needed in its defense."

Having chosen a hundred of his most active and experienced men Archie set out for the north. Crossing the Forth above Stirling, he marched through Perth and across the Carse of Gowrie through Forfar on to Montrose. Here he left his band, and taking with him only William Orr, both being attired in peasants' dress, followed the coast till he reached Dunottar.

The castle, which was of great strength, stood in a little bay with a fishing village nestled beside it.

"'Tis a strong place, William, and, if well provisioned, might hold out against an army for months. and as supplies could be thrown in by sea it could only be captured by battering down its solid walls by machines."

"'Tis indeed a strong place, Sir Archie," William Orr replied, "and it were assuredly better to slip in by the gates than to climb over the walls; but after the captures of so many of their strongholds by sudden surprise, we may be sure that a careful watch will be kept."

"Doubtless they are shrewdly on guard against surprise," Archie said; "but as they know that the king and his host are just now crossing the border into Cumberland, they may well think that for a time they are safe from disturbance. 'Tis in that that our best chance lies."

Entering the village they purchased some fish

from the fisherm e, and asking a few careless questions about the garrison, found that it was composed of one hundred and fifty men, and that extreme precautions were taken against surprise. The gates were never opened save to allow parties to pass in and out, when they were instantly closed and the drawbridge raised. Only ten of the garrison at a time were ever allowed to leave the castle, and these must go out and come in together, so that the gates should not be opened more than twice a day.

"They generally come out," the man said, at eleven o'clock and go in at four; at eleven o'clock all with corn, wood, and other stores for the castle must present themselves, so that the drawbridge need only be lowered at those times. The governor, Sir John Morris, swears that he will not be caught asleep as were those of Linlithgow and Castle Douglas. I fear," he concluded, "that we of Dunottar will be the last in Scotland to be free from the English yoke."

"That is as it may be. Other castles have been captured, and maybe the lion of Scotland may float on those walls ere long."

The man looked keenly at him.

"Methinks there is meaning in your words," he said, "and your language does not accord with your attire. I ask no questions; but be sure that should an attempt be made, there are a score of strong fellows among us who will be ready to strike a blow for freedom."

"Is that so?" Archie replied; "then, man, tak-ing you to be a true Scot, I will tell you that the attempt will be made, and that soon, and that, if you will, you can aid the enterprise. I am Sir Archibald Forbes, of whom, perhaps, you have heard."

"Assuredly," the man said in a tone of deep re-pect, "every Scotsman knows the name as that of one of the king's truest and bravest knights."

"My purpose is this," Archie said. "On a dark night some ninety-five of my men will march hither; I need a faithful friend to meet them outside the village to lead them in, and to hide them away in the cottages, having already arranged beforehand with their owners to receive them. I, myself, with four of my men will come hither in a fishing-boat well laden with fish; we will choose a time when the wind is blowing, and will seem to have been driven here by stress of weather and disabled. Then I shall try to sell our cargo for the use of the garrison. As we carry it in we shall attack the guard, and at the signal those hidden will rush out and cross the drawbridge."

"The plan is a good one," the fisherman said; "its difficulty mainly lies in the fact that the draw-bridge will be raised the moment you have crossed it, and long before your followers could arrive it would be high in the air, and you would be cut off from all aid. It never remains down for an instant after men have passed over it."

"That adds to the difficulty," Archie said thoughtfully; " but I must think of some plan to overcome it. Do you quietly go about among those you can surely trust and arrange for them to be ready to open their doors and take my men in without the slightest noise which might attract the sentries on the walls. So long as the wind is quiet and the sea smooth we shall not come, but the first day that the wind blows hard you may expect us. Then do you go out on the south road and wait for my party half a mile from the village. If they come not by midnight, return home and watch the following night."

"I understand," the fisherman said, "and will do as you bid me; and when the time comes you can rely upon twenty stout fellows here in addition to your own force."

"'Tis nigh eleven," Archie said, looking at the sun, "and we will be off at once, as the soldiers will soon be coming out, and it were best that the governor did not hear that two strangers were in the village. Vigilant as he is, a small thing might excite his suspicion and add to his watchfulness."

Archie and William Orr returned to Montrose, and there the former made an arrangement with the master of a large fishing-boat to keep his vessel ready to put to sea at any moment.

Three weeks passed without any change in the weather; then the wind began to rise and the aspect of the sky betokened a storm. William Orr at once set out with ninety-five men for Dunottar. Archie went down to the port and purchased a

large quantity of fish which had been brought in
that morning in various boats, and had it placed on
board the craft that he had hired. Then he with
four of his followers the strongest and most determined of his retainers, dressed as fishermen, went
on board and the boat at once put to sea, having,
besides Archie and his men, the master and his two
hands. The main body had started on foot at ten
in the morning, but it was late in the afternoon
before the boat put out, as Archie wished to arrive
in broad daylight next morning.

The wind was on the shore, and the boat was
sorely tossed and buffeted. Ere next morning,
showing but a rag of sail, she ran into Dunottar
harbor. They had had great difficulty in keeping
off the coast all night, and the play had nigh turned
into a tragedy, so narrow had been their escape of
being cast ashore. The bulwarks were washed
away, and the boat was in a sore plight as it drew
alongside the little quay. Assuredly no suspicion
would occur to any who saw her enter that aught
save stress of weather had driven her in.

It was twelve o'clock in the day when they
reached the port. Most of the inhabitants had
come down to the water-side to see the storm-
beaten craft enter, and among them were some
soldiers of the garrison. Archie bade four of his
men remain below, so that the unusual number of
hands should attract no attention. One of the first
to come on board was the fisherman with whom
Archie had spoken.

"Your men are all here," he said in a low tone to Archie, "and are stowed away in the cottages. Everything went well, and there was not the slightest noise."

Archie now went on shore and entered into conversation with one of the soldiers.

"Think you," he said, "that the governor would buy my cargo of fish? I have a great store on board, for I had good luck before the storm suddenly broke upon me just as I was leaving the fishing-grounds for Montrose. The gale may last for some days, and my boat will need repairs before I put to sea, therefore my fish will be spoiled before I can get them to market, and I will make a good bargain with the governor if he will take them from me."

"I should think that he will do so gladly," the soldier said, "for he can salt them down, and they make a pleasant change. How much have you got?"

"About ten baskets full," Archie replied, "of some hundred pounds each."

"I will go with you to the castle," the soldier said. "The governor will lower the drawbridge for no man, but you can speak with the warder across the moat and he will bear your message to the governor, and should he agree, you must present yourself with your men with the fish at four o'clock, at which time the drawbridge will be lowered for us to return to the castle."

Archie accompanied the soldier to the end of the

drawbridge, and parleyed with the warder. The latter acquainted the governor that the master of the fishing boat which had been driven in by stress of weather would fain dispose of his cargo of fish on cheap terms, and returned for answer that the governor would give sixpence for each basket of a hundred pounds. Archie grumbled that he should receive thrice that sum at Montrose; still that as he must sell them or let them spoil, he accepted the offer, and would be there with the fish at four o'clock.

He then returned to the boat, his ally, the fisherman, taking word round to the cottages that at four o'clock all must be in readiness to sally out on the signal, and that William Orr was to dress half a dozen of his men in fishermen's clothes and saunter up carelessly close to the castle, so as to be able to rush forward on the instant.

At the appointed hour Archie, accompanied by his four followers, each of whom carried on his shoulder a great basket filled with fish, stepped on to the quay and made their way to the castle. By the side of the moat facing the drawbridge the ten English soldiers who had been out on leave for the day were already assembled.

"Are you all there?" the warder asked.

"Yes," Archie said, "but I shall have to make another two trips down to the boat, seeing that I have ten baskets full and but four men to carry them."

"Then you must bring another load," the warder

said, "when the drawbridge is lowered to-morrow. You will have to stop in the castle to-night, and issue out at eleven to-morrow, for the governor will not have the drawbridge lowered more than twice a day."

"I would fain return to my boat," Archie said, "as I want to be at work on the repairs; but if that be the rule I must needs submit to it."

The drawbridge was now lowered. The soldiers at once stepped on to it. The four pretended fishermen had set down their baskets, and now raised them on their shoulders again. One of them apparently found it a difficult task, for it was not until Archie and his comrades were half across the drawbridge that he raised it from the ground. As he did so he stumbled and fell, the basket and its contents rolling on to the ground.

"You must wait until the morning," the warder called; "you are too late to enter now."

The man lay for a moment where he had fallen, which was half on the drawbridge, half on the ground beyond it.

"Now, then," the warder called sharply, "make haste; I am going to raise the drawbridge."

The man rose to his feet with a shout just as the drawbridge began to rise. He had not been idle as he lay. As he fell he had drawn from underneath his fisherman's frock a stout chain with a hook at one end and a large ring at the other. This he had passed round one of the chains by which the draw-bridge was raised, then under the beam on which it

rested when down, and had fastened the hook in
the ring.

Surprised at the shout, the warder worked the
windlass with extra speed, but he had scarcely
given a turn when he found a sudden resistance.
The chain which the fisherman had fixed round the
end prevented the bridge from rising. As the man
had shouted, Archie and his three comrades were
entering the gate. Simultaneously they emptied
their baskets before them. Concealed among the
fish were four logs of wood; two were three feet
long, the full depth of the baskets, two were short
wedge-shaped pieces. Before the soldiers in front
had time even to turn round, the two long pieces
were placed upright in the grooves down which the
portcullis would fall, while the two wedge-shaped
pieces were thrust into the jamb of the gate so as to
prevent it from closing. Then the four men drew
long swords hidden beneath their garments and fell
upon the soldiers.

CHAPTER XXVI.

EDINBURGH.

So VIGILANT was the watch in the castle of Dun-ottar that the instant the cry of alarm rose almost simultaneously from the warder above and the soldiers at the gate, the portcullis came thundering down. It was caught, however, by the two upright blocks of wood, and remained suspended three feet above the sill. The armed guards at the gate instantly fell upon Archie and his companions, while others endeavored in vain to close the gates. Scarcely had the swords clashed when the man who had chained down the drawbridge joined Archie, and the five with their heavy broadswords kept at bay the soldiers who pressed upon them; but for only a minute or two did they have to bear the brunt of the attack unsupported, for William Orr and the five men who had been loitering near the moat dashed across the bridge, and passing under the portcullis joined the little band.

The alarm had now spread through the castle, and the governor himself, followed by many of his men, came rushing down to the spot shouting furious orders to the warder to raise the drawbridge, being

in ignorance that it was firmly fixed at the outer
end.

Archie and his followers were now hotly pressed,
but soon a thunder of steps was heard on the drawbridge, and the whole of the band, together with
some twenty or thirty of the fishermen, passed
under the portcullis and joined them. Archie now
took the offensive, and bearing down all opposition
burst with his men into the courtyard.

The combat was desperate but short. The
governor with some of his soldiers fought stoutly,
but the suddenness of the surprise and the fury and
vigor with which they were attacked shook the
courage of many of the soldiers. Some, instead of
joining in the fray, at once threw away their arms
and tried to conceal themselves, others fought
feebly and half-heartedly, and the cries of "A
Forbes! A Forbes! Scotland! Scotland!" rose
louder and louder as the assailants gradually beat
down all resistance. In ten minutes from the falling of the portcullis all resistance was virtually
over. The governor himself fell by the hand of
Archie Forbes, and at his death those who had
hitherto resisted threw down their arms and called
for quarter. This was given, and the following day
the prisoners were marched under a strong guard
down to Montrose, there to be confined until orders
for their disposal were received from the king. For
the next fortnight Archie and his retainers, aided
by the whole of the villagers, labored to dismantle
the castle. The battlements were thrown down into

the moat, several wide breaches were made in the walls, and large quantities of straw and wood piled up in the keep and turrets. These were then fired, and the castle of Dunottar was soon reduced to an empty and gaping shell. Then Archie marched south, and remained quietly at home until the term of rest granted him by the king had expired.

Two girls and a son had by this time been born to him, and the months passed quietly and happily away until Bruce summoned him to join, with his retainers, the force with which Randolph had sat down before Edinburgh Castle. Randolph was delighted at this accession of strength. Between him and Douglas a generous rivalry in gallant actions continually went on, and Douglas had scored the last triumph. The castle of Roxburgh had long been a scource of trouble to the Scots. Standing on a rocky eminence on the margin of the Teviot, just at its junction with the Tweed and within eight miles of the border, it had constituted an open door into Scotland, and either through it or through Berwick the tides of invasion had ever flowed. The castle was very strongly fortified, so much so that the garrison, deeming themselves perfectly safe from assault, had grown careless. The command-ant was a Burgundian knight, Gillemin de Fienne. Douglas chose Shrove Tuesday for his attack. Being a feast-day of the church before the long lenten fast the garrison would be sure to indulge in conviviality and the watch would be less strict than usual. Douglas and his followers, supplied with scaling-laders, crept on all-fours toward the walls. The night was still and they could hear the sentries' conversation. They had noticed the objects advancing, but in the darkness mistook them for the cattle of a neighboring farmer. Silently the ladders were fixed and mounted, and with the dreaded war-cry, " A Douglas ! A Douglas !" the assailants burst into the castle, slaying the sentries and pouring down upon the startled revelers. Fienne and his men fought gallantly for a time, but at length all surrendered, with the exception of the governor himself and a few of his immediate followers, who retired into a tower, where they defended themselves until the following day ; then Fienne being seriously wounded, the little party also surrendered. As Douglas had no personal quarrel with the garrison of Roxburgh such as he bore with those who occupied his ancestral castle, he abstained from any unnecessary cruelties, and allowed the garrison to withdraw to England, where Fienne soon afterward died of his wounds. The castle was as usual leveled to the ground, and as the stronghold of Carlaverock soon afterward surrendered, the districts of Tweeddale and Galloway were now completely cleared of the English, with the exception of the castle of Jedburgh, which they still held.

Randolph had been created Earl of Moray, and after establishing himself in his new earldom he had returned with his feudal followers and laid siege to Edinburgh, whose castle was considered all but impregnable. It had been in the possession of the

English ever since it was captured by Edward I. in 1296, and was strongly garrisoned and well provisioned.

Even when joined by Archie Forbes and his retainers Randolph felt that the castle could not be captured by force. The various attempts which he made were signally foiled, and it was by stratagem only that he could hope to carry it. The news of the capture of Roxburgh by Douglas increased his anxiety to succeed. Accompanied by Archie he rode round the foot of the steep rock on which the castle stands, eagerly scanning its irregularities to see if by any possibility it could be scaled.

" I would give a brave reward," he said to Archie, " to any who could show us a way of climbing those rocks, which, methinks, even a goat could scarcely manage to ascend."

" I can tell you of a way," a Scotch soldier who was standing a few paces off when he made the remark said, saluting the earl. " It needs a sure foot and a stout heart, but I can lead a score of men with such qualifications to the foot of yonder walls," and he pointed to the castle rising abruptly from the edge of the rocks.

" If you can make good your word, my brave fellow," Randolph said, " you may ask your own reward, and I pledge you my word, that if it be aught in reason it shall be granted. But who are you, and how did it come that you know of a way where none is supposed to exist ?"

" My name is William Francus," the soldier said.

"I was at one time, before the king took up arms, a soldier in the castle there. I had a sweetheart in the town, and as my turn to go out from the castle came but slowly I used at night to steal away to visit her. I found after great search that on the face of yonder wall where it looks the steepest, and where in consequence but slight watch is kept, a man with steady foot and head could make shift to climb up and down, and thus, if you please, will I guide a party to the top of the rock."

"It looks impossible," Randolph said, gazing at the precipice; "but as you tell me that you have done it others can do the same. I will myself follow your guidance."

"And I," Archie said.

"What, Sir Archie, think you is the smallest number of men with whom, having once gained footing on the wall, we may fight our way to the gates and let in our friends."

"I should think," Archie replied, "that with thirty men we might manage to do so. The confusion in the garrison will be extreme at so unexpected a surprise, and if we divide in two parties and press forward by different ways they will think rather of holding together and defending themselves than of checking our course, and one or other of the parties should surely be able to make its way to the gates."

"Thirty let it be then," Randolph said. "Do you choose fifteen active and vigilant men from among your retainers; I will pick as many from mine, and as there is no use in delaying let us carry out the enterprise this very night; of course the rest of our men must gather near the gates in readiness to rush in when we throw them open."

As soon as it was dark the little party of adventurers set out on their way. Francus acted as guide, and under his leading they climbed with vast difficulty and no little danger up the face of the precipice until they reached a comparatively easy spot, where they sat down to recover their breath before they prepared for the final effort.

They could hear the sentries above speaking to each other, and they held their breath when one of them, exclaiming suddenly, "I can see you!" threw down a stone from the battlement, which leaped, crashing down the face of the rock close beside them. Great was their relief when a loud laugh from above told them that the sentry had been in jest, and had but tried to startle his comrade; then the two sentries, conversing as they went, moved away to another part of the walls.

The ascent was now continued, and proved even more difficult than that which they had passed. They were forced continually to halt, while those in front helped those following them, or were themselves hoisted up by the men behind. At last, panting and breathless, they stood on the summit of the rock, on a narrow ledge, with the castle wall rising in front of them. They had, with enormous difficulty, brought up a light ladder with them. This was placed against the wall. Francus was the first to mount, and was followed by Sir Andrew Grey, whom Randolph had invited to be of the party, by Archie Forbes and by the earl. Just as the latter stepped on to the battlements the sentries caught sight of them and shouted:

"Treason! treason! to arms!" An instant stir was heard in the castle. Rapidly the thirty men followed each other up the ladder, and so soon as the last had gained the battlements they divided in three bodies, each headed by one of the leaders. One party descended straight into the castle and there attacked the soldiers who were hurrying to arms, while the others ran along the wall in opposite directions, cutting down the sentries and brushing aside all opposition until together they met at the gate. This was thrown open, and the Scots outside running up at the top of their speed poured into the castle. At first Randolph's party, which had descended into the courtyard, had been hotly pressed, and had with difficulty defended themselves; but the attention of the startled garrison was distracted by the shouts upon the walls, which told that other parties of their assailants had gained footing there. All sorts of contradictory orders were issued. One commanded them to cut down the little party opposed to them, another ordered them to hurry to the walls, a third to seize the gate and see that it was not opened. The confusion reached its height as the Scots poured in through the open gate. The garrison, surprised and confounded as they were at this, to them, almost magical seizure of the castle by their foes, fought bravely until the governor and many of the officers were killed. Some of the men threw down their arms, and others, taking advantage of their knowledge of the castle, made their way to the gate and escaped into the open country.

The news of the capture was immediately sent to the king, by whose orders the castle and walls were razed to the ground, and thus another of the strongholds, by whose possession the English were enabled to domineer over the whole of the surrounding country, was destroyed.

While Douglas and Randolph were thus distinguishing themselves Edward Bruce captured the castle of Rutherglen, and afterward the town of Dundee; and now, save Stirling Castle, scarcely a hold in all Scotland remained in English hands. Thus was Scotland almost cleared of the invader, not by the efforts of the people at large, but by a series of the most daring and hazardous adventures by the king himself and three or four of his knights, aided only by their personal retainers. For nine years they had continued their career unchecked, capturing castle by castle and town by town, defeating such small bodies of troops as took the field against them, England, under a supine and inactive king, giving itself up to private broils and quarrels, while Scotland was being torn piecemeal from her grasp.

After Edward Bruce had captured Dundee he laid siege to Stirling. As this castle had for many months resisted Edward I. backed by the whole power of England Bruce could make little impression upon it with the limited appliances at his disposal. From February till the 24th of June the investment continued, when the governor, Sir Philip Mowbray, becoming apprehensive that his provisions would not much longer hold out, induced Edward Bruce to agree to raise the siege on condition that if by the 24th of June next, 1314, the castle was not effectually relieved by an English force, it should then be surrendered.

No satisfactory explanation has ever been given of the reasons which induced Edward Bruce to agree to so one-sided a bargain. He had already invested the place for four months, there was no possibility of an army being collected in England for its relief for many months to come, and long ere this could arrive the garrison would have been starved into surrender. By giving England a year to relieve the place he virtually challenged that country to put forth all its strength and held out an inducement to it to make that effort, which internal dissension had hitherto prevented. The only feasible explanation is that Edward Bruce was weary of being kept inactive so long a time before the walls of the fortress which he was unable to capture, and that he made the arrangement from sheer impatience and thoughtlessness and without consideration of the storm which he was bringing upon Scotland. Had it been otherwise he would surely have consulted the king before entering upon an agreement of such extreme importance.

Bruce, when he heard of this rash treaty, was highly displeased, but he nevertheless accepted the terms, and both parties began at once their preparations for the crowning struggle of the war. The English saw that now or never must they crush out the movement which, step by step, had wrested from them all the conquests which had been won with such vast effort under Edward I.; while Bruce saw that a defeat would entail the loss of all that he had struggled for and won during so many years.

King Edward issued summonses to the whole of the barons of England and Wales to meet him at Berwick by the 11th of June with all their feudal following, while the sheriffs of the various counties and towns were called upon to supply twenty-seven thousand foot-soldiers. The English of the settlements in Ireland were also summoned, besides O'Connor, Prince of Connaught, and twenty-five other native Irish chiefs, with their following, all of whom were to be under the command of Richard de Burgh, Earl of Ulster.

The Prince Bishop of Constance was requested to furnish a body of mounted crossbowmen. A royal fleet of twenty-three vessels was appointed to assemble for the purpose of operating on the east coast, while the seaports were commanded to fit out another fleet of thirty vessels. A third fleet was ordered to assemble in the west, which John of Lorne was appointed to command under the title of High-admiral of the Western Fleet of England. From Aquitaine and the French possessions the

vassals were called upon to attend with their men-
at-arms, and many knights from France, Gascony,
and Germany took part in the enterprise.

Thus, at the appointed time, over one hundred
thousand men assembled at Berwick, of whom forty
thousand were men-at-arms, and the rest archers
and pikemen. For the great armament the most
ample arrangements were made in the way of warlike stores, provisions, tents, and means of transport,
together with the necessary workmen, artificers,
and attendants.

This army surpassed both in numbers and equipments any that Edward I. had ever led into Scotland, and is considered to have been the most numerous and best equipped that ever before or since
has gathered on English ground. Of the whole of
the great nobles of England only four were absent
—the Earls of Warrenne, Lancaster, Arundel, and
Warwick—who, however, sent their feudal arrays
under the charge of relations.

Among the leaders of this great army were the
Earls of Gloucester, Pembroke, Hereford, and An-
gus, Lord Clifford, Sir John Comyn, Sir Henry
Beaumont, Sir John Seagrave, Sir Edmund Morley,
Sir Ingram de Umfraville, Sir Marmaduke de
Twenge, and Sir Giles de Argentine, one of the
most famous of the Continental knights.

While this vast army had been preparing, Bruce
had made every effort to meet the storm, and all
who were loyal and who were able to carry weapons
were summoned to meet at Torwood, near Stirling,

previous to the 24th of June. Here Edward Bruce,
Sir James Douglas, Randolph, Earl of Moray, Walter the Steward, Angus of Isla, Sir Archibald
Forbes, and a few other knights and barons assembled with thirty thousand fighting men, besides
camp-followers and servants. It was a small force
indeed to meet the great army which was advancing against it, and in cavalry in particular it was
extremely weak. The English army crossed the
border, and marched by Linlithgow and Falkirk
toward the Torwood.

Each army had stirring memories to inspire it, for
the English in their march crossed over the field
of Falkirk, where sixteen years before they had
crushed the stubborn squares of Wallace; while
from the spot which Bruce selected as his battle-
ground could be seen the Abbey Craig, overlooking
the scene of the Scottish victory of Stirling Bridge.
On the approach of the English the Scotch fell back
from the Torwood to some high ground near Stirling now called the New Park. The lower ground,
now rich agricultural land called the Carse, was
then wholly swamp. Had it not been so, the position
now taken up by Bruce would have laid the road to
Stirling open to the English.

The Scotch army was divided into four divisions.
The center was commanded by Randolph. Edward
Bruce commanded the second, which formed the
right wing. Walter the Steward commanded the
left wing, under the guidance of Douglas, while the
king himself took command of the fourth division,

which formed the reserve, and was stationed in rear
of the center in readiness to move to the assistance
of either of the other divisions which might be hard
pressed. The camp-followers, with the baggage
and provisions, were stationed behind the Gillies
Hill.

The road by which the English would advance
was the old Roman causeway running nearly north
and south. The Bannock Burn was fordable from
a spot near the Park Mill down to the village of
Bannockburn. Above, the banks were too high and
steep to be passed; while below, where ran the
Bannock through the carse, the swamps prevented
passage. The army was therefore drawn up, with
its left resting on the sharp angle of the burn above
the Park Mill, and extended where the villages of
Easterton, Borestine, and Braehead now stand to
the spot where the road crosses the river at the
village of Bannockburn. In its front, between it
and the river, were two bogs, known as Halberts
Bog and Milton Bog, while, where unprotected by
these bogs, the whole ground was studded with deep
pits; in these stakes were inserted, and they were
then covered with branches and grass. Randolph's
center was at Borestine, Bruce's reserve a little
behind, and the rock in which his flagstaff was
placed during the battle is still to be seen. To
Randolph, in addition to his command of the center
division, was committed the trust of preventing any
body of English from passing along at the edge of
the carse, and so making round to the relief of
Stirling.

On the morning of Sunday, the 23d of June, immediately after sunrise, the Scotch attended mass, and confessed as men who had devoted themselves to death. The king, having surveyed the field, caused a proclamation to be made that whosoever felt himself unequal to take part in the battle was at liberty to withdraw. Then, knowing from his scouts that the enemy had passed the night at Falkirk, six or seven miles off, he sent out Sir James Douglas and Sir Robert Keith with a party of horsemen to reconnoiter the advance.

The knights had not gone far when they saw the great army advancing, with the sun shining bright on innumerable standards and pennons, and glistening from lance-head, spear, and armor. So grand and terrible was the appearance of the army that upon receiving the report of Douglas and Keith the king thought it prudent to conceal its full extent, and caused it to be bruited abroad that the enemy, although numerous, was approaching in a disorderly manner.

The experienced generals of King Edward now determined upon making an attempt to relieve Stirling Castle without fighting a pitched battle upon ground chosen by the enemy. Had this attempt been successful, the great army, instead of being obliged to cross a rapid stream and attack an enemy posted behind morasses, would have been free to operate as it chose, to have advanced against the strongholds which had been captured by the Scots, and to force Bruce to give battle upon ground of their choosing. Lord Clifford was therefore despatched with eight hundred picked men-at-arms to cross the Bannock beyond the left wing of the Scottish army, to make their way across the carse, and so to reach Stirling. The ground was, indeed, impassable for a large army; but the troops took with them fagots and beams, by which they could make a passage across the deeper parts of the swamp and bridge the little streams which meandered through it.

As there was no prospect of an immediate engagement, Randolph, Douglas, and the king had left their respective divisions, and had taken up their positions at the village of St. Ninians, on high ground behind the army, whence they could have a clear view of the approaching English army. Archie Forbes had accompanied Randolph, to whose division he, with his retainers, was attached. Randolph had with him five hundred pikemen, whom he had withdrawn from his division in order to carry out his appointed task of seeing that the English did not pass along the low ground at the edge of the carse behind St. Ninians to the relief of Stirling; but so absorbed were knights and men-at-arms in watching the magnificent array advancing against the Scottish position that they forgot to keep a watch over the low ground. Suddenly one of the men, who had straggled away into the village, ran up with the startling news that a large party of English horse had crossed the corner of the carse, and had already reached the low ground beyond the church.

" A rose has fallen from your chaplet, Randolph," the king said angrily.

Without a moment's loss of time Randolph and Archie Forbes set off with the spearmen at a run, and succeeded in heading the horsemen at the hamlet of Newhouse. The mail-clad horsemen, confident in their numbers, their armor and horses, laid their lances in rest, struck spurs into their steeds, and, led by Sir William Daynecourt, charged down upon the Scotch spearmen. Two hundred of these consisted of Archie Forbes' retainers, all veterans in war, and who had more than once, shoulder to shoulder, repelled the onslaught of the mailed chivalry of England. Animated by the voices of their lord and Randolph, these, with Moray's own pikemen, threw themselves into a solid square, and, surrounded by a hedge of spears, steadily received the furious onslaught of the cavalry. Daynecourt and many of his men were at the first onslaught unhorsed and slain, and those who followed were repulsed. Again and again they charged down upon the pikemen, but the dense array of spears was more than a match for the lances of the cavalry, and as the horses were wounded and fell, or their riders were unhorsed, men rushed out from the square, and with axe and dagger completed the work. Still the English pressed them hard, and Douglas, from the distance, seeing how hotly the pikemen were pressed by the cavalry, begged the

king to allow him to go to Randolph's assistance.
Bruce, however, would suffer no change in his position, and said that Randolph must stand or fall by
himself. Douglas, however, urged that he should
be allowed to go forward with the small body of
retainers which he had with him. The king consented, and Douglas set off with his men.

When the English saw him approach they recoiled
somewhat from the square, and Douglas, being now
better able to see what was going on, commanded
his followers to halt, saying that Randolph would
speedily prove victorious without their help, and
were they now to take part in the struggle they
would only lessen the credit of those who had
already all but won the victory. Seeing the enemy
in some confusion from the appearance of the rein-
forcement, Randolph and Archie now gave the word
for their men to charge, and these, rushing on with
spear and axe, completed the discomfiture of the
enemy, killed many, and forced the rest to take
flight. Numbers, however, were taken. Randolph
is said to have had but two men killed in the
struggle.

CHAPTER XXVII.

BANNOCKBURN.

AFTER the complete defeat of the party under
Lord Clifford, and the failure of their attempt to
relieve Stirling, Randolph and Douglas returned
together to the king. The news of their success
spread rapidly, and when Randolph rode down from
St. Ninians to his division, loud cheers broke from
the whole Scottish army, who were vastly encour-
aged at so fair a commencement of their struggle
with the English.

The English army was still advancing slowly,
and Bruce and his leaders rode down to the front of
the Scottish line, seeing that all was in order and
encouraging the men with cheering words. When
the English army approached the stream King
Edward ordered a halt to be sounded for the purpose of holding a council, whether it was best to
encamp for the night or at once to advance against
the enemy. The Earls of Gloucester and Hereford, who commanded the first division, were so far
ahead that they did not hear the sound of the
trumpet, and continuing their onward march
crossed the Bannock Burn and moved on toward

the Scotch array. In front of the ranks of the
defenders the king was riding upon a small palfrey,
not having as yet put on his armor for the battle.
On his helmet he wore a purple cap surmounted by
a crown. Seeing him thus within easy reach, Sir
Henry de Bohun, cousin of the Earl of Hereford,
laid his lance in rest and spurred down upon the
king. Bruce could have retired within the lines of
his soldiers; but confident in his own prowess, and
judging how great an effect a success under such
circumstances would have upon the spirits of his
troops, he spurred forward to meet his assailant
armed only with his axe. As the English knight
came thundering down, the king touched his palfrey with his spur, and the horse, carrying but a
light weight, swerved quickly aside; De Bohun's
lance missed his stroke, and before he had time
to draw rein or sword, the king, standing up in
his stirrups, dealt him so tremendous a blow
with his axe as he passed, that it cleft through
helmet and brain, and the knight fell dead to the
ground.

With a shout of triumph the Scotch rushed for
ward and drove the English advance-guard back
across the stream; then the Scotch leaders led their
men back again to the position which they had
quitted, and re-formed their array. Douglas,
Edward Bruce, Randolph, and Archie Forbes now
gathered round the king and remonstrated with him
on the rashness of an act which might have proved
fatal to the whole army. The king smiled at such

Bruce slays Sir Henry de Bohun.—Page 452.

—In Freedom's Cause.

remonstrances from four men who had, above all others, distinguished themselves for their rash and daring exploits, and shrugging his shoulders observed only that it was a pity he had broken the shaft of his favorite axe.

The English array now withdrew to a short distance, and it became evident that the great battle would be delayed till the morrow. The Scotch army therefore broke its ranks and prepared to pass the night on the spot where it stood. The king assembled all his principal leaders round him, and after thanking God for so fair a beginning of the fight as had that day been made, he pointed out to them how great an effect the two preliminary skirmishes would have upon the spirits of both armies, and expressed his confidence in the final result. He urged upon them the necessity for keeping their followers well in hand, and meeting the charges of the enemy's horse steadily with their spears; and especially warned them, after repulsing a charge, against allowing their men to break their array either to plunder or take prisoners, so long as the battle lasted, as the whole riches of the English camp would fall into their hands if successful. He pledged himself that the heirs of all who fell should have the succession of their estates free from the usual feudal burdens on such occasions.

The night passed quietly and in the morning both armies formed their array for battle. Bruce, as was customary, conferred the honor of knighthood upon several of his leaders. Then all proceeded to their allotted places and awaited the onset. Beyond the stream and extending far away toward the rising ground were the English squadrons in their glittering arms, the first division in line, the others in heavy masses behind them. Now that the Scotch were fairly drawn up in order of battle, the English could see how small was their number in comparison with their own, and the king in surprise exclaimed to Sir Ingram de Umfraville:

"What! will yonder Scots fight us?"

"That verily will they," the knight replied, for he had many a time been engaged in stout conflict with them, and knew how hard it was even for mail-clad knights to break through the close lines of Scottish spears. So high a respect had he for their valor, that he urged the king to pretend to retire suddenly beyond the camp, when the Scots, in spite of their leaders, would be sure to leave their ranks and flock into the camp to plunder, when they might be easily dispersed and cut to pieces. The king, however, refused to adopt the suggestion, saying, that no one must be able to accuse him of avoiding a battle or of withdrawing his army before such a rabble.

As the armies stood confronting each other in battle array a priest passed along the Scottish front, crucifix in hand, exhorting all to fight to the death for the liberty of their country. As he passed along the line each company knelt in an attitude of prayer. King Edward, seeing this, exclaimed to Sir Ingram:

"See yonder folk kneel to ask for mercy!"

"Ay, sire," the knight said, looking earnestly at the Scots, "they kneel and ask for mercy, but not of you; it is for their sins they ask mercy of God. I know these men, and have met and fought them, and I tell you that assuredly they will win or die, and not even when death looks them in the face will they turn to fly."

"Then if it must be so," said the king, "let us charge."

The trumpet sounded along the line. First the immense body of English archers crossed the burn and opened the battle by pouring clouds of arrows into the Scottish ranks. The Scotch archers, who were in advance of their spearmen, were speedily driven back to shelter beyond their line, for not only were the English vastly more numerous, but they shot much further and more accurately. And now the knights and men-at-arms, on their steel clad horses, crossed the burn. They were aware of the existence of Milton Bog, which covered the Scottish center, and they directed their charge upon the division of Edward Bruce on the Scottish right. The crash as the mailed horses burst down upon the wood of Scottish spears was tremendous. Bruce's men held firm, and the English in vain strove to break through their serried line of spears. It was a repetition of the fight of the previous day, but on a greater scale. With lance and battle-axe the chivalry of England strove to break the ranks of the Scotch, while with serried lines of spears, four deep, the Scotch held their own. Every horse which, wounded or riderless, turned and dashed through the ranks of the English, added to the confusion. This was much further increased by the deep holes into which the horses were continually falling, and breaking up all order in their ranks. Those behind pressed forward to reach the front, and their very numbers added to their difficulty.

The English were divided into ten divisions or "battles," and these one by one crossed the stream with banners flying, and still avoiding the center followed the line taken by the first and pressed forward to take part in the fray.

Randolph now moved with the center to the support of the hardly pressed right, and his division, as well as that of Edward Bruce, seemed to be lost among the multitude of their opponents. Stewart and Douglas moved their division to the right and threw themselves into the fray, and the three Scottish divisions were now fighting side by side, but with a much smaller front than that which they had originally occupied. For a time the battle raged furiously without superiority on either side. The Scotch possessed the great advantage that, standing close together in ranks four deep, every man was engaged, while of the mounted knights and men-at-arms who pressed upon them, only the front line was doing efficient service. Not only, therefore, was the vast numerical superiority of the English useless to them, but actually a far larger number of the Scottish than of themselves were using their weapons in the front rank, while the great proportion of the English remained helplessly behind their fighting line, unable to take any part whatever in the fight. But now the English archers came into play again, and firing high into the air rained their arrows almost perpendicularly down upon the Scottish ranks. Had this continued it would have been as fatal to the Scots at Bannockburn as it was at Falkirk; but happily the Scottish horse told off for this special service were here commanded by no traitors, and at the critical moment the king launched Sir Robert Keith, the mareschal of Scotland, against the archers with five hundred horsemen. These burst suddenly down upon the flank of the archers and literally swept them before them. Great numbers were killed, others fell back upon the lines of horsemen who were ranged behind, impatient to take their share in the battle; these tried to drive them back again, but the archers were disheartened, and retreating across the stream took no further part in the battle. The charge of the Scottish horse should have been foreseen and provided against by placing strong bodies of men-at-arms on the flanks of the archers, as these lightly armed troops were wholly unable to withstand a charge by cavalry.

The Scottish archers, now that their formidable opponents had left the field, opened a heavy fire over the heads of the pikemen upon the horsemen surrounding the squares, and when they had shot away their arrows, sallied out and mingled in the confused mass of the enemy, doing tremendous ex-

ecution with their axes and knives. Hitherto the
king had kept his reserve in hand; but now that
the English archers were defeated and their horsemen in inextricable confusion, he moved his division
down and joined in the mêlée, his men shouting his
well-known battle-cry.

Every Scotch soldier on the field was now engaged. No longer did the battle-cries of the various
parties rise in the air. Men had no breath to waste
in shouting, but each fought silently and desperately
with spear or axe, and the sound of clanging blows
of weapons, of mighty crash of sword or battle-axe
on steel armor, with the cries and groans of wounded
men were alone heard. Over and over again the
English knights drew back a little so as to gain speed
and impetus, and flung themselves on the Scottish
spears, but ever without effect, while little by little
the close ranks of the Scotch pressed forward until,
as the space between their front and the brook nar-
rowed, the whole of the English divisions became
pent up together, more and more incapable of using
their strength to advantage. The slaughter in their
front divisions had already been terrible. Again
and again fresh troops had taken the places of those
who had formed the front ranks, but many of their
best and bravest had fallen. The confusion was too
great for their leaders to be able to direct them
with advantage, and seeing the failure of every
effort to break the Scottish ranks, borne back by
the slow advance of the hedge of spears, harassed
by the archers who dived below the horses, stabbing

them in their bellies, or rising suddenly between them to smite down the riders with their keen, heavy, short-handled axes, the English began to lose heart, and as they wavered the Scotch pressed forward more eagerly, shouting: " On them ! on them ! They give way ! they give way !"

At this critical moment the servants, teamsters, and camp-followers who had been left behind Gillies Hill, showed themselves. Some of their number from the eminence had watched the desperate struggle, and on hearing how their soldiers were pressed by the surrounding host of English men-at arms they could no longer remain inactive. All men carried arms in those days. They hastily chose one of their own number as leader, and fastening some sheets to tent-poles as banners, they advanced over the hill in battle array, and moved down to join their comrades.

The sight of what they deemed a fresh division advancing to the assistance of the Scotch brought to a climax the hesitation which had begun to shake the English, and ensured their discomfiture. Those in rear turned bridle hastily, and crossing the Bannock Burn, galloped away. The movement so begun spread rapidly, and although those in front still continued their desperate efforts to break the line of Scottish spears, the day was now hopelessly lost. Seeing that this was so, the Earl of Pembroke seized the king's rein and constrained him to leave the field with a bodyguard of five hundred horse. Sir Giles de Argentine, who had hitherto remained by the king's side, and who was esteemed the third best knight in Europe—the Emperor Henry of Luxemberg and Robert Bruce being reckoned the two best—bade farewell to the king as he rode off.

"Farewell, sire," he said, "since you must go, but I at least must return; I have never yet fled from an enemy, and will remain and die rather than fly and live in disgrace."

So saying, the knight spurred down to the conflict, and charged against the array of Edward Bruce, and there fell fighting valiantly. The flight of the king and his attendants was the signal for a general rout. Great numbers were slain, many men were drowned in the Forth, and the channel of the Bannock was so choked with the bodies of dead men and horses that one could pass over dry-shod. The scattered parties of English were still so numerous that Bruce held his men well in hand until these had yielded themselves prisoners. Douglas was charged to pursue the king, but he could only muster sixty horsemen. A short distance from the field he met a Scottish baron, Sir Laurence Abernethy, with twenty-four men-at-arms, on his way to join the English, for even as yet but few of the Scottish nobles were on the side of the king. Upon hearing what had happened, Sir Laurence, with the easy facility which distinguished the Scottish nobles of the period, at once changed sides, swore fealty to Bruce, and joined Douglas in the pursuit of his late friends. They overtook the king's party at Linlithgow, but Pembroke kept his men well together, and while still retiring, showed so bold an appearance that Douglas did not venture to charge. Finally the English reached the castle of Dunbar, where the king and his immediate attendants were received by his ally, Earl Patrick of Dunbar. So cowed were the fugitives that they left their horses outside the castle gate, and these were captured by their pursuers. The main body of the king's bodyguard continued their way in good order, and reached Berwick in safety. Edward gained England in a fishing-boat from Dunbar. Eighteen years had elapsed since his father had entered Scotland with an army deemed sufficient for its entire subjugation; had sacked and destroyed the rich and prosperous town of Berwick, routed the army of Baliol, marched through Scotland, and, as he believed, permanently settled his conquest. Now the son had lost all that his father had won.

Among the fugitive remains of the English army were a considerable body of Welsh, who, being lightly armed, fled at full speed toward the border, but being easily distinguished by their white dresses and the absence of defensive armor, almost all were slain by the peasantry. The Earl of Hereford, the Earl of Angus, Sir John Seagrave, Sir Anthony Lucy, Sir Ingram de Umfraville, with a great number of knights, six hundred men-at-arms, and one thousand infantry, keeping together, marched south toward Carlisle.

As they passed Bothwell Castle, which was held by the governor for England, the earls and knights entered the castle, their followers remaining without; but the governor, on hearing the result of the battle, closed the gates and took all who had entered prisoners, and, changing sides, handed them over to Bruce. Their followers continued their march south, but were for the most part slain or taken prisoners before they reached the border.

When all resistance had ceased on the field the victors collected the spoil. This consisted of the vast camp, the treasures intended for the payment of the army, the herds of cattle, and stores of provisions, wine, and forage; the rich wearing apparel and arms of the knights and nobles killed or made prisoners, many valuable horses, and the prisoners who would have to be ransomed, among whom were twenty-two barons and sixty knights. The spoil was estimated at £200,000, equal to £3,000,000 of money in these days. The king refused to take any share in this plunder, dividing it wholly among his troops. Thirty thousand English lay dead on the field, including two hundred knights and seven hundred esquires, and among the most distinguished of the dead were the Earl of Gloucester, Sir Giles de Argentine, Lord Robert Clifford, Sir Edmund Manley, seneschel of England, Sir William de Mareschal, Sir Payne Tybtot, and Sir John Comyn. Sir Marmaduke de Twenge was among the prisoners.

Bruce's conduct to his prisoners was even more honorable to himself than was the great victory that he had won. In spite of his three brothers, his brother-in-law Seaton, his friends Athole and Fraser, having

been executed by the English, and the knowledge
that their mangled remains were still exposed over
London Bridge and the gates of Carlisle and New-
castle—in spite of the barbarous and lengthened captivity of his wife, his sister and daughter, and his
friend the Countess of Buchan—in spite of the conviction that had he himself been made prisoner he
would at once have been sent to the scaffold—Bruce
behaved with a magnanimity and generosity of the
highest kind. Every honor was paid to the English
dead, and the bodies of the chief among these were
sent to their relatives in England, and the prisoners
were all either ransomed or exchanged. Sir Marmaduke de Twenge was dismissed free of ransom
and loaded with gifts, and even the Scotch nobles,
such as Sir Philip Mowbray, who were taken fighting in the ranks of their country's enemy, were
forgiven. This noble example exercised but little
influence upon the English. When Edward Bruce
was killed four years afterward at Dundalk in
Ireland, his body was quartered and distributed, and
his head presented to the English king, who bestowed
upon Bermingham—who commanded the English
and sent the gift to him—the dignity of Earl of
Louth.

Among the prisoners was Edward's poet-laureate,
Baston, a Carmelite friar, who had accompanied the
army for the purpose of writing a poem on the
English victory. His ransom was fixed at a poem
on the Scotch victory at Bannockburn, which the
friar was forced to supply.

With Bannockburn ended all hope on the part of the English of subjugating Scotland; but the war continued fitfully for fourteen years, the Scotch frequently invading England and levying heavy contributions from the northern counties and towns, and the English occasionally retaliating by the same process; but at length peace was signed at Northampton.

In 1315 a parliament assembled at Ayr for the purpose of regulating the succession to the throne. It was then agreed that in case of the king's death without male issue his brother Edward should succeed to it, and that if Edward left no heirs, the children of Marjory, the king's daughter, should succeed. Shortly afterward Marjory was married to Walter the Steward. Edward Bruce was killed unmarried. A son was afterward born to the king, who reigned as David II., but having died without issue, the son of Marjory and the Steward became king. The hereditary title of Steward was used as the surname for the family, and thus from them descended the royal line of Stewart or Stuart, through which Queen Victoria at present reigns over Great Britain, Ireland, and their vast dependencies.

After Bannockburn Archie Forbes went no more to the wars. He was raised to the dignity of Baron Forbes by the king, and was ever regarded by him as one of his most trusty councillors, and his descendants played a prominent part in the changing and eventful history of Scotland; but the

proudest tradition of the family was that their
ancestor had fought as a patriot by the side of
Bruce and Wallace when scarce a noble of Scotland
but was leagued with the English oppressors of
their country.